MASTERING PRODUCTS LIABILITY

CAROLINA ACADEMIC PRESS MASTERING SERIES

RUSSELL WEAVER, SERIES EDITOR

For other titles, please go to caplaw.com.

Mastering Administrative Law, Second Edition
Linda D. Jellum

Mastering Adoption Law and Policy
Cynthia Hawkins DeBose

Mastering Alternative Dispute Resolution
Kelly M. Feeley, James A. Sheehan

Mastering Appellate Advocacy and Process, Second Edition
Donna C. Looper, George W. Kuney

Mastering Art Law, Second Edition
Herbert Lazerow

Mastering Bankruptcy
George W. Kuney

Mastering Civil Procedure, Fourth Edition
David Charles Hricik

Mastering Constitutional Law, Second Edition
John C. Knechtle, Christopher J. Roederer

Mastering Contract Law
Irma S. Russell, Barbara K. Bucholtz

Mastering Corporate Tax, Second Edition
Gail Levin Richmond, Reginald Mombrun, Felicia Branch

Mastering Corporations and Other Business Entities, Second Edition
Lee Harris

Mastering Criminal Law, Third Edition
Ellen S. Podgor, Cynthia E. Jones, Peter J. Henning,
Neil P. Cohen, Sanjay K. Chhablani

**Mastering Criminal Procedure, Volume 1:
The Investigative Stage, Third Edition**
Peter J. Henning, Cynthia E. Jones, Ellen S. Podgor,
Karen McDonald Henning, Sanjay K. Chhablani

**Mastering Criminal Procedure, Volume 2:
The Adjudicatory Stage, Third Edition**
Peter J. Henning, Cynthia E. Jones, Ellen S. Podgor,
Karen McDonald Henning, Sanjay K. Chhablani

Mastering Elder Law, Third Edition
Ralph C. Brashier

Mastering Employment Discrimination Law, Third Edition
Jeffrey M. Hirsch, Joseph A. Seiner, Sandra F. Sperino

Mastering Environmental Law
Joel A. Mintz, Tracy D. Hester

Mastering Evidence
Ronald W. Eades

Mastering Family Law
Janet Leach Richards

Mastering First Amendment Law
John C. Knechtle

Mastering Income Tax, Second Edition
Gail Levin Richmond, Christopher M. Pietruszkiewicz

Mastering Intellectual Property
George W. Kuney, Donna C. Looper

Mastering International Sales Law
Herbert Lazerow

Mastering Interviewing and Counseling
Kelly M. Feeley, Rebecca C. Morgan

Mastering Labor Law
Paul M. Secunda, Anne Marie Lofaso, Joseph E. Slater, Jeffrey M. Hirsch

Mastering Legal Analysis and Communication
David T. Ritchie

Mastering Legal Analysis and Drafting, Second Edition
George W. Kuney, Donna C. Looper

Mastering Legislation, Regulation, and Statutory Interpretation, Third Edition
Linda D. Jellum

Mastering Native American Law, Third Edition
Angelique Wambdi EagleWoman, Stacy L. Leeds

Mastering Negotiable Instruments (UCC Articles 3 and 4) and Other Payment Systems, Second Edition
Michael D. Floyd

Mastering Negotiation
Michael R. Fowler

Mastering Partnership Taxation
Stuart Lazar

Mastering Products Liability, Second Edition
Tim Kaye

Mastering Professional Responsibility, Second Edition
Grace M. Giesel

Mastering Property Law, Second Edition
Darryl C. Wilson

Mastering Sales
Colin P. Marks, Jeremy Kidd

Mastering Secured Transactions: UCC Article 9, Third Edition
Grace M. Giesel

Mastering Tort Law, Third Edition
Russell L. Weaver, Edward C. Martin, Andrew R. Klein,
Paul J. Zwier, II, John H. Bauman

Mastering Trademark and Unfair Competition Law, Second Edition
Lars S. Smith, Llewellyn Joseph Gibbons

Mastering Trusts and Estates, Second Edition
Gail Levin Richmond

MASTERING PRODUCTS LIABILITY

SECOND EDITION

Tim Kaye

PROFESSOR OF LAW
STETSON UNIVERSITY COLLEGE OF LAW

CAROLINA ACADEMIC PRESS
Durham, North Carolina

LIBRARY OF CONGRESS CATALOGING-IN-PUBLICATION DATA

Names: Kaye, Tim, 1961- author.
Title: Mastering products liability / Tim Kaye.
Other titles: Products liability law
Description: Second edition. | Durham, North Carolina : Carolina Academic Press, 2025. | Series: Mastering series | Includes bibliographical references and index.
Identifiers: LCCN 2025017986 | ISBN 9781531032050 (paperback) | ISBN 9781531032067 (ebook)
Subjects: LCSH: Products liability--United States.
Classification: LCC KF1296 .K39 2025 | DDC 346.7303/8--dc23/eng/20250411
LC record available at https://lccn.loc.gov/2025017986

Carolina Academic Press
700 Kent Street
Durham, North Carolina 27701
(919) 489-7486
www.cap-press.com

Printed in the United States of America

CONTENTS

SERIES EDITOR'S FOREWORD

The Carolina Academic Press *Mastering* Series is designed to provide you with a tool that will enable you to easily and efficiently "master" the substance and content of law school courses. Throughout the series, the focus is on quality writing that makes legal concepts understandable. As a result, the series is designed to be easy to read and is not unduly cluttered with footnotes or cites to secondary sources.

In order to facilitate student mastery of topics, the *Mastering* Series includes a number of pedagogical features designed to improve learning and retention. At the beginning of each chapter, you will find a "Roadmap" that tells you about the chapter and provides you with a sense of the material that you will cover. A "Checkpoint" at the end of each chapter encourages you to stop and review the key concepts, reiterating what you have learned. Throughout the book, key terms are explained and emphasized. Finally, a "Master Checklist" at the end of each book reinforces what you have learned and helps you identify any areas that need review or further study.

We hope that you will enjoy studying with, and learning from, the *Mastering* Series.

Russell L. Weaver
PROFESSOR OF LAW &
DISTINGUISHED UNIVERSITY SCHOLAR
UNIVERSITY OF LOUISVILLE,
LOUIS D. BRANDEIS SCHOOL OF LAW

PREFACE

My colleague, Lou Virelli, suggested that I write this book. It was written to the sound of Daniela, Paulina, and Alejandra Villarreal, collectively known as The Warning, whom I am delighted to support on Patreon.

I should also like to thank the exceptionally smart Ashley Gregory for reading and commenting on earlier drafts of what became chapters 1 to 4. She made numerous excellent suggestions, though we will never agree on the use of conjunctions! All errors and infelicities of expression that remain are, of course, of my own making and not hers.

Other exceptionally intelligent people contributed in their own ways, perhaps even without realizing it. Bob Bickel remains a constant source of encouragement for everything I do. Matt DiMasso ensures that my mind is constantly broadened, even if I sometimes wish it weren't. Helen Driscoll entertains me with tales of Portugal, house renovations, and a new spy. Gary Falasca makes sure I don't get too big for my britches, though I can now point out how badly Manchester City are playing. Anne Gary makes the most amazing baked goods. Andrea Hatton is always a breath of fresh air. Sage Iverson has caused me to know more about The Bachelor than I ever wanted. Lisa Johnston performs the most hilarious rants. Kelsey Krueger inspires me with her fearlessness and drive. Luz Nagle advocates for abused women in the Americas. Lauren Sloniger guides me through unfamiliar bits of popular culture.

Extra special thanks are due to Marguerite Boissonnault, Sharon Dearman, Nia Kaye, Abigail Lee (née Pressler), Allie Padin, and Kristina Self. To spell out precisely how much you mean to me would take too long, so I'll settle for this: I love you all.

MASTERING PRODUCTS LIABILITY

CHAPTER 1

History and Background of Products Liability

HISTORY AND BACKGROUND ROADMAP

- Understand the difference between products and services
- Be aware of the different theories of liability
- Understand the difference between fault and strict liability
- Understand who is a potential defendant
- Understand who is a potential plaintiff

1.1 What Is a Product?

As its name suggests, products liability law is the field of law that deals with liability for defective products. It seems appropriate, therefore, to start by identifying what constitutes a product and—just as important—to establish what does not.

In fact, however, there is something that needs to be understood even before we do that. It is essential to recognize that the decision about what constitutes a product is a question of law to be determined by the judge. It is emphatically *not* a question of fact to be determined by the jury. As a question of law, it is subject to the doctrine of precedent, so that the courts within a given jurisdiction will take a consistent view. This provides the necessary predictability about what the law covers.

Section 19 of the Third Restatement of Torts: Products Liability defines a product as *tangible* property that is distributed commercially. In the overwhelming majority of cases, this means that "products" are essentially the same as "goods" under section 2-105(1) of the Uniform Commercial Code. But there are some differences. For example, real property—which would never qualify as "goods"—may be considered a product if the context makes it appropriate to do so for reasons of public policy. Some states—such as Wisconsin in *Ransome v. Wisconsin Elec. Power Co.*, 87 Wis. 2d 605 (1979)—have defined electricity as a product once it has passed through the consumer's meter.

1.2 Products vs Services

The main point of defining products is that this enables them—at least in theory—to be distinguished from services.

Products are typically mass-produced and brought to market by a manufacturer who does not know the identity of the buyer or consumer, so that there is little or no opportunity for them to negotiate the terms of the transaction. Services, on the other hand, are typically designed by a seller to match a buyer's specific requirements. They therefore typically afford plenty of opportunity for negotiation about the terms of the relationship between buyer and seller.

In most cases, distinguishing between products and services is unproblematic. A doctor examining and treating a patient provides a service, while any drug they prescribe is a product. Even in the case of a surgically implanted device that dispenses microdoses of a drug at pre-programmed intervals, we can say that the surgeon provides a service, while the device and drug are either considered together as one product or separately as two products. (This distinction may be important because the manufacturer of the device may be different from the manufacturer of the medication.)

But what about a map? It is, after all, a tangible entity, but its purpose is arguably to provide a navigation service. In *Saloomey v. Jeppeson & Co.*, 707 F.2d 671 (1983), a federal court held that mass-produced maps are products in just the same way as mass-produced cans of beans. So where does that leave an app like Waze, or Google Maps? Or, indeed, any computer software?

The reason why this matters is that, in most cases, the law on faulty services is more favorable to the seller than is the law on defective products. Vendors will, therefore, often seek to classify what they are selling as services rather than products. This is one reason why software vendors typically claim that their software is not a product to be purchased, but a service for whose usage they merely grant a license. Such software cannot, however, exist without taking up physical space on a hard drive somewhere, so that raises the possibility that it might nevertheless be "tangible property that is distributed commercially" and thus a product.

More recently, such companies have switched to a model where their software is accessed from the cloud. Not for nothing is this model known as "Software as a Service" (or SaaS). One of the reasons for this shift is that the software does not reside on the user's hardware. This arguably eliminates the chance of such software being treated as a product because the user cannot claim to have purchased something tangible.

Yet it is important to remember that the question of what constitutes a product is a matter of law. It cannot be unilaterally determined by the seller (nor by the buyer, for that matter). If electricity—the medium through which the SaaS model works—may sometimes be a product, it may be that even a SaaS may be treated as a product in some circumstances.

Also as yet unresolved is the status of items that make use of, or depend on, artificial intelligence (AI) or machine learning (ML). Whether a self-driving vehicle is a product or a service might, perhaps, depend on its degree of autonomy or on the nature of the task it is performing (e.g., parking) at any given time.

Such questions highlight not just how topical products liability law often is, but also how what purports to be a question of law might still require the judge to hear significant factual evidence.

1.3 Early History

It is sometimes said that products liability law dates back to the earliest days of the United States. What such assertions typically omit, however, is the fact that the law in question was only a feature of the antebellum South, because it was designed to protect the interests of slave-buyers. If a slave was unfit to work, then the buyer would have recourse against the seller for not charging a "fair" price. In South Carolina, this led to a more general "fair price" doctrine being applied to other products too. But this was not the norm and, after the Civil War, even the courts of South Carolina abandoned the doctrine.

What replaced it was the doctrine of *caveat emptor*, which had already taken hold in the North. Literally translated as "let the buyer beware," this put the onus on the buyer to check that the product was of the desired quality and fit for purpose. In the absence of a warranty from—or fraud by—the seller, if the product subsequently proved defective, that was a loss to be borne by the buyer.

Caveat emptor remained the norm until well into the twentieth century, when a series of well-publicized cases of injuries caused by defective products caused the courts to impose greater responsibility on sellers. These new responsibilities, coupled with some elements of the older doctrines of warranty and misrepresentation, came to form what we now think of as products liability law.

1.4 Six Theories of Liability

In fact, modern products liability law now comprises six discrete legal theories:

- Breach of warranty;
- Misrepresentation;
- Negligence;
- Manufacturing defects;
- Design defects; and
- Failures to warn.

This means that it is frequently possible for a plaintiff to frame a case in several different ways. Sometimes these alternatives may appear to be just different ways of saying much the same thing. But each boasts its own requirements, defenses, and remedies, so that not every theory will be available in every case.

These differences mean that some theories will be more attractive to a plaintiff than others. But one theory cannot be said always to be preferable for a plaintiff than another; that is very much a matter of the specific context of the case at hand. Conversely, a defendant may sometimes argue that the plaintiff has pleaded a case using an inappropriate theory so that, unless the judge grants leave to amend, the plaintiff's case should fail. It is, therefore, essential to understand the requirements of each theory.

1.5 Contracts vs Torts

One obvious difference is that warranty law is part of the law of contracts, whereas the other theories of liability are all part of the law of torts. Bearing in mind that it is always the plaintiff who has the initial opportunity to frame the case, this is significant for two reasons.

The first is that cases pleaded in contracts require proof of privity between the plaintiff and defendant. Without such a relationship, the defendant cannot be said to owe any contractual duties to the plaintiff. This presents no problem for the plaintiff if they bought the product direct from the defendant, but the typical product purchase involves a consumer buying from a retailer who did not make the product. Similarly problematic for traditional privity analysis are work-based product liability cases, where an employee may be injured by a tool purchased by their employer.

Privity does not, however, have any role to play in torts cases. In many cases, therefore, pleading a case in torts provides a way for the plaintiff to circumvent the need to prove privity (though, as we shall see, the law of contracts has also expanded its view of what constitutes privity beyond traditional bounds).

Secondly, while punitive damages may be available in cases where a tort is proved, such a remedy is not available for suits in contracts. This clearly has the potential to make pleading a case in torts more attractive to a plaintiff, but it should not be over-emphasized. Despite the cases that make the headlines, most product liability cases do not lead to an award of punitive damages.

Even when a punitive damages award is made, it will almost always trigger an appeal. With the prospect of such litigation dragging on for a long time, the true effect of a punitive damages award is typically to encourage the parties to settle. The defendant then pays less than the original amount awarded, while the plaintiff receives this admittedly smaller sum much earlier than they would do if the litigation were to continue.

1.6 Fault vs Strict Liability

An associated distinction is that between different levels of culpability (or fault).

Claims in contracts require no proof that the defendant intended to break the contract, nor that they were reckless or negligent in doing so. Liability in contracts stems from the breach alone without any need to prove fault. We call this "strict" liability.

In a breach of warranty claim, the plaintiff needs to prove that the product did not match up to the warranty given. But since such claims fall within the province of the law of contracts, there is no necessity to establish that the reason for its failure to do so was because of the fault of the defendant. In other words, liability for breach of warranty is strict.

The law of torts, by contrast, categorizes torts into three groups. In descending order of culpability, these are as follows:

- Intentional torts;
- Torts involving unreasonable behavior; and
- Strict liability torts.

As the most egregious form of tortious conduct, intentional torts are by far the most likely to attract an award of punitive damages. At the same time, they are also the hardest to prove because it is exceptionally difficult to establish what the state of mind of the defendant was at the time when the wrongdoing occurred.

For the purposes of products liability law, the only theory that *requires* proof of bad intent is fraudulent misrepresentation. Nevertheless, a plaintiff may also allege intent in cases of manufacturing defects, design defects, and failures to warn not because it is necessary to win the case but in order to encourage the jury to make an award of punitive damages.

Until *MacPherson v. Buick Motor Co.*, 217 N.Y. 382 (1916), the only grounds for a claim in what we now call products liability law were a breach of warranty—involving strict liability in contracts—or misrepresentation, involving intentional liability in torts. *MacPherson*, however, established that claims in torts could also be brought if injury from a defective product resulted from the defendant's unreasonable conduct, i.e., negligence.

In *Greenman v. Yuba Power Products, Inc.*, 377 P.2d 897 (Cal. 1963), the Supreme Court of California expanded tortious liability even further by recognizing strict products liability *in torts*, where privity was no longer required but something equivalent to a contractual warranty nevertheless attached itself to the product. The justification for this expansion was that if *both* plaintiff and defendant are blame-free, the defendant manufacturer or distributor is much more likely to be able to bear the cost of any injury sustained, because it either has significantly more resources or it has access to liability insurance. It is *Greenman* that is considered to mark the birth of modern products liability law.

Over the course of the next thirty years, this notion of strict products liability splintered into three different theories—manufacturing defects, design defects, and failures to warn—while attitudes in favor of strict liability in torts experienced significant challenge. These days, while liability for manufacturing defects is still typically treated as strict, liability for a failure to warn has been re-established as requiring either negligence or intent.

At the same time, design defects have become a battleground. Defendants point to the Third Restatement of Torts: Products Liability as authority for the proposition that such liability once again requires proof of some degree of fault. Plaintiffs, on the other hand, criticize the Third Restatement for not being a Restatement at all but an improper attempt to change the law. Instead, they argue that the Second Restatement of Torts, which treats products liability as strict, remains good law.

1.7 The Five Elements

Despite the many differences between each of the six theories of liability, products liability cases typically follow a highly consistent pattern that is characterized by the presence of *all* of the following five elements:

1. A product;
2. Which has been sold, or otherwise distributed, by someone in the business of selling or distributing that type of product;
3. But which was defective;
4. In a manner that has caused—or is likely to cause—personal injury or property damage;
5. To a victim who was using or consuming the product, or who was an otherwise reasonably foreseeable third party.

It should be emphasized, however, that while the presence of all of these elements is almost always *necessary* for the law to recognize the case as one that concerns products liability, such presence is not necessarily *sufficient* to sustain a verdict for the plaintiff. This is because one or more of these elements may be trumped by an appropriate affirmative defense. In other words, these are the five elements required for a *prima facie* case.

Point (1) was addressed earlier in this chapter. Point (3) is the crux of the distinctions between the six theories of liability and will be the focus of most of the rest of this book. Point (4) will be addressed in the chapter on causation. That leaves point (2), which makes it possible to identify potential defendants, and point (5), which identifies the potential plaintiffs. These are tackled in the next two sections.

1.8 Potential Defendants

It is important to appreciate that liability for defective products is not limited to product manufacturers. In fact, section 1 of the Third Restatement of Torts: Products Liability makes it clear that liability also extends to anyone engaged in the business of selling "or otherwise distributing" products, while section 20 gives that notion a very wide meaning.

Private sellers cannot normally be held liable in a products liability action, unless they sell or distribute products on such a frequent basis as to transform such conduct into the operation of a small business.

On the other hand, those engaged in "otherwise distributing" products include not just manufacturers, but also retailers and wholesalers. And those who use or provide a product as part of the performance of a commercial transaction or service (e.g., a rental car company) are also deemed to be distributors of the product concerned. In *Providence Health System v. Brown*, 372 Or. 225 (2024), for example, the Supreme Court of Oregon *en banc* found that a hospital can be a "seller" of pharmaceuticals.

Sellers and distributors of a *used* product may, in some cases, also be liable if such a product proves defective. Auctioneers, on the other hand, are not commercial distributors because, as explained in *New Texas Auto Auction Services, L.P. v. Gomez De Hernandez*, 249 S.W.3d 400, 402 (2008), they do not distribute products so much as *facilitate* their distribution.

This distinction has been litigated repeatedly in different states with Amazon as the defendant. The issue has been whether Amazon is a product distributor when it manages the delivery of products listed by private sellers on Amazon's website. Amazon has always argued that, unless it is delivering its own products, it is doing nothing more than providing logistics services and is thus a mere facilitator of distribution. The courts, however, have generally found that Amazon's degree of control over the storage and delivery of such products is enough to make it a distributor subject to products liability law.

On July 29, 2024, moreover, the United States Consumer Safety Commission (CPSC) ruled that Amazon is a product distributor for the purposes of the Consumer Product Safety Act (CPSA). While this Act has a narrower focus than common law products liability—it is primarily about imposing a duty to recall unsafe and hazardous products—the CPSC's designation may be a factor that courts take into account for products liability law more generally.

1.9 Potential Plaintiffs

There is no doubt that the product purchaser is entitled to bring a products liability claim if they are injured by that product. The more problematic issue is which victims may bring a products liability claim when they were *not* such a purchaser.

The decision of the New York Court of Appeals in *MacPherson v. Buick Motor Co.*, 217 N.Y. 382 (1916), started the courts on a journey to the position that any consumer injured by a defective product that they themselves purchased is entitled to bring a products liability claim, even if they did not purchase it direct from the manufacturer. This view was finally confirmed in *Greenman v. Yuba Power Products, Inc.*, 377 P.2d 897 (Cal. 1963).

It was *Greenman* that established that products liability law is largely a matter for the law of torts and so does not require privity of contract. Instead, the victim needs to have been a foreseeable user or consumer in order to bring a viable claim. This typically includes family members, those living in the same household as the purchaser, and those who work for—or on the premises of—the purchaser.

While the last observation *does* mean that products liability claims may arise from workplace accidents, it *does not* mean that products liability claims may be brought against the victim's employer. Such claims are covered instead by workers' compensation provisions. It *does*, however, mean that an employee may be entitled to bring a claim against the manufacturer and/or distributor of a defective product if it injures them while using it at work.

Whether innocent bystanders should also be able to bring a products liability claim after being injured despite neither using nor consuming the product in question has, however, proved a knotty problem that is typically left to be determined according to the context of each specific case.

1.10 Opening the Floodgates?

Defendants regularly argue that allowing the claim currently before the court will "open the floodgates" for numerous similar claims in the future, resulting in "crushing liability" not just for the current defendant but for all similar such organizations in future. Unfortunately, this "floodgates" claim typically conflates three rather different issues, which it is important to distinguish.

The first is the notion that "floods" of lawsuits will be brought because plaintiffs (advised, of course, by their attorneys) find that they have the opportunity to recover compensation when formerly that would not have been possible. This may be called the threat of floods of lawsuits (or floods of claims). Naturally, such a threat will arise only if a significant increase occurs in the number of plaintiffs who find that they have a realistic chance of success in seeking compensation for an injury suffered.

A second type of potential "flood" sounds superficially similar but is, in fact, quite different. It is the risk that "floods" of claims will reach the courtroom, rather than being settled through negotiation, thus causing far more work for the courts (perhaps to the extent that there will be an unmanageable backlog of cases and so the courts will be unable to cope). This may be called the threat of floods of trials.

A potential flood of trials is by no means the same sort of threat as that of a potential flood of lawsuits. In fact, if the threat of floods of lawsuits is genuine, then defendants will generally settle out of court because they will realize that there is little prospect of a successful defense. The threat of floods of trials, however, will be valid only if there is such confusion or ambiguity in the law that both plaintiffs and defendants believe that they have a reasonable chance of success in any litigation. In such circumstances, neither side may have a significant incentive to settle before trial, and so the courts would risk being flooded with more cases.

It should be easy to see why the law would much prefer to avoid a flood of trials. Ideally, we all want the law to be clear, so that both parties know where they stand and unnecessary litigation (and its associated costs of time and money) can be avoided. In practice, of course, total clarity is not always possible because of disputed facts or issues of law that had not previously been foreseen. But it is clearly in everyone's interest to avoid a flood of trials if at all possible.

The same cannot necessarily be said for the risk of floods of lawsuits. After all, it would be very strange if defendants could simply escape liability on the basis that they have injured a larger number of people rather than just one or two. If the consequence of their conduct is that they are made bankrupt, that might simply be the appropriate price to be paid (even if it also impacts other innocent people like the defendant's employees).

This is where the third type of "floodgates" argument becomes relevant. It is the threat of a flood of *frivolous* lawsuits. Again, it is clear that the courts should ensure that their rulings are sufficiently robust to ensure that such a flood does not occur. But a flood of lawsuits is not necessarily the same thing as a flood of frivolous lawsuits. The latter arises where the law is sloppily framed so that undeserving plaintiffs are able to claim compensation for harms that they have not sustained. But if a defendant's product injures many victims, there would seem to be little reason why the law should create some artificial barrier to the bringing of claims for products liability. Asbestos-related claims are a prime example.

1.11 Role of Federal Law

Both contracts and torts are fields of law that come within the purview of the states. As a result, products liability law is not typically a concern of the federal courts except by way diversity jurisdiction. There are, however, three significant exceptions to that general principle:

1. Where a case of mass torts involves multi-district litigation (MDL).
2. Where a products liability defendant enters bankruptcy protection.
3. Where a case is pre-empted by federal law.

MDLs have no effect on the substantive law involved. Despite being heard in federal court sitting in one jurisdiction, the law of the original state jurisdiction will still apply. The procedural law will often be substantially different, however, and this might have significant implications for the way such a case is litigated.

Where a defendant enters bankruptcy protection, by contrast, any lawsuit against them will be automatically stayed, as will any judgment entered against them within the previous ninety days. Any attempt to have the stay limited must be approved by the Bankruptcy Court, which is generally reluctant to do so.

Since being in financial difficulties is not a requirement of entering bankruptcy protection, it has become quite commonplace for potential defendants to products liability lawsuits to threaten to enter such protection if a claim is either brought against them or results in the award of significant damages.

Pre-emption occurs when a case concerns a matter of international or interstate commerce—thus creating federal jurisdiction—and the relevant federal rules or regulations conflict with state law. The most common instance is where a federal statute either provides immunity for a product manufacturer—such as the National Childhood Vaccine Injury Act of 1986 barring design defect claims against vaccine manufacturers—or else provides for a method of conflict resolution other than litigation in state courts.

This should not be taken as indicating that the mere existence of a federal law in the relevant field is enough to pre-empt a lawsuit in state court. On the contrary, section 4 of the Third Restatement of Torts: Products Liability makes clear that non-compliance with a federal safety statute automatically marks that product as defective for the purposes of a products liability claim. Along the same lines, it also says that compliance with such a standard is not automatically dispositive, but is simply one factor to be borne in mind as part of both the defectiveness and pre-emption inquiries.

HISTORY AND BACKGROUND CHECKPOINTS

- While the modern law of products liability was not born until the middle of the twentieth century, it had a significant gestation period in the form of the pre-existing doctrines of warranty and misrepresentation.
- There are now six theories of liability, one of which lies in the law of contracts, while the others are part of the law of torts.
- Despite the six theories of liability, the plaintiff in a products liability case typically needs to prove the same five elements in order to succeed.
- The question of whether products liability requires, or should require, proof of fault continues to be controversial and is answered differently in different states.

CHAPTER 2

Warranties

WARRANTIES ROADMAP

- Understand the difference between express and implied warranties
- Understand the implied warranties of merchantability and fitness for purpose
- Understand whether, and how, such warranties may be excluded
- Understand vertical and horizontal privity
- Develop a basic awareness of general commercial practice in the sale of goods

---

2.1 Express Contractual Warranties

As noted in Chapter 1, the doctrine of *caveat emptor*, which developed as part of the US common law over its first two hundred years or so, meant that the risks of a product being defective were, by default, borne by the buyer. Not for nothing does the Latin translate as "let the buyer beware."

Even today, the law imposes no duty on sellers to disclose flaws in the products that they are selling or distributing, so long as they do not actually act in bad faith by perpetrating a misrepresentation or fraud. Section 2-103(1)(b) of the Uniform Commercial Code (UCC) requires merely "honesty in fact and the observance of reasonable commercial standards of fair dealings in the trade."

The main exception to *caveat emptor* occurred when a seller had provided a warranty. This is, in effect, a guarantee of some aspect of the product's quality.

For decades there was confusion about what needed to be said or written to constitute a warranty, but section 2-313 of the UCC nowadays makes it clear that an express warranty can be made by "an affirmation of fact or promise," a "description of the goods," or by the provision of a sample.

The time at which any of these events occur is, however, crucial. Since a breach of warranty claim is part of the law of contracts, it is essential that the warranty be provided either at the time that the contract is formed or sometime beforehand. As the Court of Appeals of New York explained in *Hawkins v. Pemberton*, 6 Sickels 198 (N.Y. 1872), "it is a general rule that whatever a seller represents, at the time of a sale, is a warranty."

Section 2-313 is also significant in that it removed the requirement for the plaintiff to show reliance on the warranty before being able to bring a successful claim that it had been breached. Instead, the law now requires that the warranty be "part of the basis of the bargain." This means that the warranty must have been part of what the buyer was buying: not just (say) a toaster but a toaster with a two-year warranty. Again, this highlights the need for the warranty to have been provided before—or at the time of—the making of the contract. But, since there is no longer any need to show reliance, it is irrelevant whether the existence of such a warranty played a part in the purchaser's decision to buy it.

Another ramification of a warranty being recognized by the law of contracts is that, if the product fails to live up to the warranty, there is no need for the plaintiff to prove fault by the defendant. As noted in Chapter 1, liability in contracts is strict, so non-compliance is automatically a breach of warranty. Moreover, since the defendant does not need to have been at fault, there can be no defense of comparative fault. *Wickersham v. Ford Motor Co.*, 997 F. 3d 526, 540 (4th Cir. 2021).

2.1.1 Puffery

There are, nevertheless, some statements and representations that can never amount to a warranty. These are instances of what is known as "puffery": statements so silly, exaggerated, or vague that no reasonable person should be expected to rely on them.

The suggestion, for example, that women prefer men who wear a particular brand of T-shirt is classic puffery. So is a boast that a particular car is the "best we have ever built" because there is no clear criterion for what is "best."

Claims such as "your daily ray of sunshine" are also likely to be puffery because their metaphorical nature makes it virtually impossible to ascertain what such statements really mean.

2.2 Implied Contractual Warranties

Claims for breach of warranty do not have to rely on a breach of an *express* warranty. A breach of an *implied* warranty also provides a sound basis for a claim. But "implied" in this context does not mean something that may be inferred from the seller's conduct. On the contrary, it means a warranty imposed by law. The most important implied warranties for the purposes of products liability law are the implied warranty of merchantability and, where a particular purpose has been made known to the seller, the implied warranty of fitness for that particular purpose.

These implied warranties did not develop organically within the US, and they certainly do not reflect the "fair price" doctrine of antebellum South Carolina. Instead, they were taken from the Sale of Goods Act (passed in England in 1893) and written into the Uniform Sales Act of 1906, model legislation drafted by the National Conference of Commissioners on Uniform State Laws. The Uniform Sales Act was gradually adopted by a number of states and later formed the basis of the UCC, which superseded it.

2.2.1 Implied Warranty of Merchantability

Section 2-314(1) of the UCC now provides that:

> Unless excluded or modified . . . , a warranty that the goods shall be merchantable is implied in a contract for their sale if the seller is a merchant with respect to goods of that kind. Under this section the serving for value of food or drink to be consumed either on the premises or elsewhere is a sale.

This makes clear that only a "merchant with respect to goods of that kind" provides such a warranty. Section 2-104 defines a merchant as "a person that deals in goods of the kind or otherwise holds itself out by occupation as having knowledge or skill peculiar to the practices or goods involved in the transaction." Private sellers, therefore, typically fall outside the reach of the implied warranty of merchantability.

Note, however, that there is nothing in this language that restricts the identity of buyers. In other words, a buyer may be a business and still be entitled to rely on an implied warranty of merchantability just as much as a private consumer may do so.

Section 2-314(2) then sets out the criteria by which merchantability is to be judged. These involve assessing whether the item in question meets reasonable expectations of its quality, including being fit for its ordinary purpose(s), and whether it conforms to any statements made on its label or container.

Unlike an express warranty, however, an implied warranty may be modified or excluded. Section 2-316(2) provides that, to successfully modify or exclude the implied term of merchantability, the seller "must mention merchantability" and, if doing so in writing, such "writing must be conspicuous." Alternatively, if state law permits it, the seller can successfully avoid providing any implied warranties at all by using language such as: "There are no warranties which extend beyond the description on the face hereof" or by saying that the goods are provided "as is," "with all faults," or other language that is generally understood to mean that no implied warranties are provided.

Section 2-316(3)(c) provides that implied warranties may also be excluded or modified through a course of dealing.

An important difference between express warranties and the implied warranty of merchantability is that, while reliance is irrelevant to the existence of the former, it is very much relevant to the existence of the latter. Section 2-316(3)(b) thus treats the implied warranty of merchantability as having been excluded if, before purchasing the item, the buyer either fully inspected it or refused to carry out an inspection that would have revealed the defect.

2.2.2 Implied Warranty of Fitness for Particular Purpose

Unlike the implied of warranty of merchantability, section 2-315 of the UCC makes clear that the implied warranty of fitness for a particular purpose can come into existence only if the buyer initiates a dialog with the seller. In the course of that dialog, they must explain that, after purchasing the item, they intend to use it for a purpose other than that for which it was originally intended. If the seller then confirms that the product will be suitable for such a purpose, they will have provided an implied warranty of fitness for that particular purpose if the "the buyer [relies] on the seller's skill or judgment" when choosing the product.

At least, that will be the case unless they have also taken steps to modify or exclude the provision of such warranties. Section 2-316(2) of the UCC specifies that such a modification or exclusion must be in "writing and conspicuous" unless one of the options discussed above to avoid providing *any* implied warranties is used instead.

2.2.3 Interplay Between Express and Implied Warranties

As the courts became comfortable with recognizing the presence of express and implied warranties, the attention of businesses has turned to using the former as a means of effectively denying the latter. In other words, it has become standard practice to draft standard express warranties in a manner designed to limit or exclude implied warranties. As Judge Francis put it in *Henningsen v. Bloomfield Motors, Inc.*, 32 N.J. 358, 375 (1960):

> Warranties developed in the law in the interest of and to protect the ordinary consumer.... But the ingenuity of the Automobile Manufacturers Association, by means of its standardized form, has metamorphosed the warranty into a device to limit the maker's liability.

Over sixty years later, Judge Francis's words remain true. Just as in *Henningsen* itself, contracts for the purchase of a car still typically involve an express warranty that provides a "limited warranty" while excluding the implied warranty of merchantability. Warranties accompanying other products often work in a similar manner.

2.2.4 Unconscionability

It might be thought that such practices are unfair and, indeed, section 2-719 of the UCC does make contractual limitations on damages for personal injury "prima facie unconscionable". Moreover, section 2-302 states that if a court finds that a contractual term is unconscionable, it "may refuse to enforce the contract, or it may enforce the remainder of the contract without the unconscionable clause, or it may so limit the application of any unconscionable clause as to avoid any unconscionable result."

But these provisions do not impinge on section 2-316, which specifically allows a seller to indicate that they are not providing a warranty in the first place. The combined effect of the various UCC provisions on express and implied warranties and exclusions is essentially that:

1. It is permissible, through appropriate language, to avoid providing any express or implied warranties; but
2. Where such warranties are provided, it is not possible to exclude or limit damages for personal injury caused by their breach.

2.2.5 Magnuson Moss Warranty Act

There is, however, another statute that does limit the power of businesses who wish to avoid providing warranties. It is the federal Magnuson Moss Warranty Act. This requires that any warranty must be described as either "full" or "limited," be written in a style that is easy to understand, and be available where the product in question is sold so that a consumer may read it before buying the item. A product may be accompanied with both a full and a limited warranty, provided that they are, according to 15 U.S.C. § 2308, "clearly and conspicuously differentiated."

More pertinent for present purposes, though, is that the Act also includes a prohibition, 15 U.S.C. § 2308(a), on a supplier disclaiming or modifying "any implied warranty to a consumer with respect to [a] consumer product" if the supplier either provides "any written warranty" about the product or, "at the time of sale, or within 90 days thereafter, ... enters into a service contract with the consumer" in relation to the product. In other words, if an express warranty is supplied, the implied warranty of merchantability (and, if applicable, the implied warranty of fitness for a particular purpose) cannot be denied.

The one exception to this is identified by section 2308(b), which allows for implied warranties to be limited in duration "to the duration of a written warranty of reasonable duration, if such limitation is conscionable and is set forth in clear and unmistakable language and prominently displayed on the face of the warranty."

It should now be clear how the language and effect of limited warranties offered with automobiles came to be as it is.

2.3 Relaxing Privity

Henningsen also made a significant modification to traditional contract law. The plaintiff, Mrs. Henningsen, was not the person who had bought the defective vehicle. Despite her husband having bought the vehicle from a dealer, it was she who brought suit against the manufacturer, Chrysler.

According to traditional contract law, even if it could be argued that the husband was acting as agent for his wife, there was no privity between plaintiff and defendant. On that basis, only the dealer could be liable as the only person in contractual privity with Mr. and Mrs. Henningsen. The traditional view would thus have seen the manufacturer responsible for constructing the dangerous car escaping liability, because (a) there cannot be a breach of warranty if there is no contract to which the warranty attaches, and (b) there can be no such contract without privity.

The Supreme Court of New Jersey held, nevertheless, that when a manufacturer puts a product into the stream of trade, "an implied warranty that it is reasonably suitable for use ... accompanies it into the hands of the ultimate purchaser." *Henningsen v. Bloomfield Motors, Inc.*, 32 N.J. 358, 384 (1960).

2.3.1 Collateral Warranties

At first glance, it might appear that the court failed to follow well-established contract doctrine. Further analysis, however, reveals a different story. In fact, *Henningsen* is best understood as exemplifying a transaction involving not one but two contracts. One involved the purchase of the vehicle: we may call this the "main" contract. But there was also a second contract between Chrysler and the Henningsens for the provision of a warranty. This latter contract ran alongside and was dependent on the main contract. Indeed, it could not exist without the main contract, for otherwise there would be no goods to warrant. For this reason, we call the second contract a "collateral" contract.

It might now be objected that the Henningsens had provided no consideration for such a collateral contract. Judge Francis disagreed: "The consideration for this warranty is the purchase of the manufacturer's product from the dealer by the ultimate buyer."

In other words, the real significance of *Henningsen* is that, instead of treating a warranty simply as an element within a contract for the sale of goods, it treats a warranty as being capable of forming the basis of a contract in its own right, albeit that this contract is collateral to the main contract. While the warranty remains "part of the basis of the bargain," that "bargain" encompasses the whole transaction involving manufacturer, retailer, and ultimate user or consumer.

One effect of this approach is to make it possible for both a retailer and a manufacturer to offer their own warranties on the same product. The consumer can then choose to make use of whichever is more favorable at the time of a defect in the product manifesting itself, and may even choose to make use of different warranties at different times.

2.3.2 Vertical and Horizontal Privity

Although collateral warranty might seem to provide a means of circumventing the requirement for privity, what it actually does is emphasize the need for *two* instances of privity to co-exist. These have come to be known as vertical and horizontal privity.

Horizontal privity is the traditional type that exists between the buyer and seller of a product. In *Henningsen*, Mr. and Mrs. Henningsen were in horizontal privity with the car dealership. So horizontal privity is the essence of the main contract.

Vertical privity, on the other hand, is the type of privity that extends up the chain of distribution. There would be vertical privity between, for example, a manufacturer and a wholesaler or between a wholesaler and retailer. In *Henningsen*, there was vertical privity between Chrysler and the car dealership.

The significance of a collateral contract lies in the courts' readiness to relax the requirement of vertical privity. Applying it strictly would mean that a victim could bring an action for breach of warranty only against the retailer from whom they purchased the product. Recognition of a collateral contract, by contrast, widens the ambit of vertical privity so as to permit the recognition of some sort of contractual relationship between the manufacturer and the consumer.

This is despite the fact that they do not directly do business with each other and are, instead, somewhat "remote" from each other. Nevertheless, according to this approach, a consumer may pursue a claim for breach of warranty against the manufacturer directly.

Such recognition of a contractual relationship between a remote purchaser—here, the Henningsens—and a remote seller—here, Chrysler—has not been universally adopted by the states. Indeed, a proposal in 2003 to amend the UCC to insert new provisions that would have standardized this approach was withdrawn because it was deemed too controversial. In many jurisdictions, the ability to sue on the basis that a product failed to meet the terms of a collateral warranty is more properly framed as a form of liability in torts.

2.3.3 "Lemon" Laws

So far as automobiles are concerned, legislation in many states has, in any event, outpaced the UCC in the form of so-called "lemon" laws. These laws typically apply to new or demonstrator motor vehicles which manifest defects during their first two years of use.

If, after a reasonable number of attempts to repair such defects, the vehicle still fails to meet the claims made for it under the manufacturer's warranty, the manufacturer is then required either to refund the purchase price or to provide a replacement vehicle.

Yet lemon laws have significant limitations so far as products liability is concerned. They are designed to ensure that the purchaser gets what they paid for, but they provide no recourse if someone is injured as a result of one of the vehicle's defects.

2.4 Third Party Beneficiaries

Disagreement over vertical privity was somewhat reminiscent of prior disagreement among the states over horizontal privity. As already noted, this is the type of privity that a buyer has with a retail seller. But what if the person injured by the defective product is not the person who bought it? Can such horizontal privity be extended to include others besides the original purchaser?

Henningsen itself extended privity to the buyer's spouse on the basis of the well-known doctrine of spousal agency, where one spouse is presumed to act on behalf of the other. But what if (say) the victim had been one of their adult children, who was driving the car with their permission? This raises the question of how far horizontal privity should extend.

The UCC adopts the same approach as *Henningsen* and focuses on how close of a relationship the victim has with the purchaser. As would later occur in the context of the discussions over vertical privity, however, there was no agreement about what should count as a sufficiently close relationship. But, unlike the later vertical privity proposal, they found agreement in compromise, so that section 2-318 of the UCC contains three alternative provisions.

The most restrictive alternative, Alternative A, has been the one to have found most favor among the states. This extends horizontal privity:

> to any natural person who is in the family or household of his buyer or who is a guest in his home if it is reasonable to expect that such person may use, consume or be affected by the goods.

Alternative B goes further and applies "to any natural person who may reasonably be expected to use, consume or be affected by the goods." Alternative C goes further still by enabling non-natural persons, such as corporations, to claim horizontal privity, even if they did not themselves purchase the product in question.

Whichever alternative has been adopted in a given state, sellers "may not exclude or limit" that extension of horizontal privity. And such privity applies to both express and implied warranties. Yet the differences between the alternatives are crucial. An employee who is injured by defective equipment purchased by her employer will have no claim under Alternative A because they cannot be said to be a either a family member or guest of the employer.

In the 1970s and 1980s, several courts found that employees should be considered part of the employer's "family," but that view finds much less favor today on the grounds that (a) they should seek to bring a claim in the law of torts instead, and (b) that would eliminate much of the difference between Alternative A and Alternative B.

2.5 Contracts vs Torts Revisited

It cannot be overemphasized that warranties are part of the law of contracts. Contract law has always been primarily about an economic transaction rather than a means of seeking compensation for physical injury. And, as has already been noted, there are two major disadvantages with bringing a claim in contracts.

First, there is the need to prove privity, and this sometimes requires proof not only of horizontal privity but also of vertical privity. Secondly, there is the lack of availability of punitive damages.

Yet there are three circumstances where suing for breach of warranty may be more advantageous to a plaintiff than bringing a claim within the ambit of the law of torts. Together these mean that a plaintiff will often include a claim for breach of warranty in contracts alongside claims made in torts.

2.5.1 Limitation Period

The first advantage is that the period of time in which a plaintiff must bring a claim—known as a "limitation period" or as a "statute of limitation" because it is set by statute—is typically longer for a claim of breach of contract than the equivalent period for a claim brought in the law of torts. According to section 2-725 of the UCC, for example, an action must be brought within four years of when the breach occurs (though this period may be reduced by agreement to no less than one year), whereas it is common for states to set limitations periods in torts as short as one or two years.

While this naturally makes no practical difference if a case is brought expeditiously, it has significant ramifications for plaintiffs who delayed before consulting an attorney. Ironically, it is typically those who tried hardest to avoid litigation who often end up shooting themselves in the foot by trying to deal with their situation by themselves.

Since the limitation period runs from the date of breach, it is important to establish when that breach occurs. Section 2-725(2) sets the default date of breach as the date on which delivery was tendered. If, however, a "warranty explicitly extends to future performance of the goods" so that it will be necessary to wait to see if the product lives up to those claims, then "the cause of action accrues when the breach is or should have been discovered."

Kenworth of Indianapolis v. Seventy-Seven, 134 N.E.3d 370 (Ind. 2019), illustrates this principle. It was undisputed that the limitations period in that case had been set at one year. What was disputed was when the limitations period was triggered. The Supreme Court of Indiana noted that the warranty said that the trucks to which it applied "*will be* free from defects" for 12-months/100,000-miles (emphasis added). Use of the future tense rather than past or present tense indicated that the "warranty explicitly extend[ed] to future performance of the goods" under 2-725(2) of the UCC and so the limitation period was not triggered until "the breach [was] or should have been discovered."

2.5.2 Harm to the Defective Product Itself

The second advantage is where the harm sustained includes harm to the defective product itself. While this might appear to be a case of property damage, and so satisfies the fourth of the five elements required to establish a *prima facie* case of products liability, the law actually considers that to be a form of economic loss. This is because, whether the product harms itself or not, the product has simply failed to provide the value expected.

Once classified as economic loss, it is inevitably subject to what is known as the "economic loss rule" in torts. This states that the defendant cannot be liable to pay damages to compensate for purely economic losses. *See, e.g.*, *Ponzio v. Mercedes-Benz USA, LLC*, 447 F. Supp. 3d 194 (D.N.J. 2020).

So, unlike physical harm caused to other property or to humans, harm sustained by the defective product itself cannot be compensated through the law of torts. Such compensation can, however, be obtained through the law of contracts, because that compensation is designed to provide or restore the value that the buyer expected to receive from the contract. Thus, a product with an electrical fault that causes the whole product to be burned out will form the basis for a breach of warranty claim—specifically, for breach of the implied warranty of merchantability—in contracts for the price of a replacement item, as well as a claim in either contracts or torts for any other harm that the fire caused.

2.5.3 Loss of Profits

It is sometimes easy to forget that plaintiffs in a products liability case are not limited to private consumers. They may also include an individual running a business or even a corporation. The case of *Kenworth of Indianapolis v. Seventy-Seven*, 134 N.E.3d 370 (Ind. 2019), for example, arose from the sale of forty dump trucks. Indeed, Alternative C in section 2-318 of the UCC expressly recognizes the possibility of businesses bringing products liability claims.

If a product manifests a defect in the working environment (*e.g.*, by catching fire), it may cause the business concerned to lose profits while the item is repaired or replaced. Lost profits are self-evidently a form of economic loss and so are subject to the economic loss rule. The third advantage of bringing a claim for breach of warranty in contracts is that it again avoids that rule and thus permits claims for loss of profits.

It is true that courts are prepared to relax the rule for claims of loss of profits in torts where the parties are in a "special" relationship. But this requires that the buyer be heavily dependent on the seller's professional expertise in a manner similar to the way that a business depends on its accountant to file taxes on time. Such a relationship is typically much more applicable to contracts for services than to contracts for the sale of goods.

So, while there isn't the absolute prohibition on bringing claims for loss of profits in torts in the same way that there is for claims relating to harm sustained by the defective product itself, claims for loss of profits in torts remain highly problematic. Such claims can, however, be brought without issue as breach of warranty claims in the law of contracts.

2.5.4 Limitations on Damages

Classifying harm to the defective product itself as economic loss rather than physical harm has another significant ramification. This may be seen where the contract includes a clause that purports to limit or exclude the amount of damages for which the seller may be liable for a breach of warranty.

Section 2-719 of the UCC permits such a limitation or exclusion "unless the limitation or exclusion is unconscionable." It then goes on to add that: "Limitation of consequential damages for injury to the person in the case of consumer goods is *prima facie* unconscionable," whereas "limitation of damages where the loss is commercial is not."

Thus, the major reason for framing a products liability claim as a breach of warranty—the ability to recover compensation for the harm done to the defective item itself—may legitimately be limited or excluded altogether. This might seem to undermine the whole argument for bringing such a claim, but that would be to overstate the matter. In fact, section 2-718 requires that any such limitation must be "reasonable in the light of the anticipated or actual harm caused by the breach, the difficulties of proof of loss, and the inconvenience or nonfeasibility of otherwise obtaining an adequate remedy."

WARRANTIES CHECKPOINTS

- Warranty law is part of the law of contracts and thus requires privity.
- Privity may be divided into horizontal and vertical; in some cases, both are required.
- Warranties may be express or implied.
- An express warranty must be part of the basis of the bargain and requires one of the following:
  - an affirmation of fact or promise;
  - sale by sample; or
  - sale by description.

- The implied warranties are those of merchantability and fitness for a particular purpose.
- The implied warranty of merchantability requires that the product is sold by a merchant and is fit for its ordinary purposes.
- The implied warranty of fitness for a particular purpose requires that the seller knows of that purpose and the buyer relies on the seller's skill or judgment when choosing the product.
- Implied warranties may be limited or excluded only in specific circumstances, and never if a written, express warranty is provided.
- The economic loss rule means that compensation for damage to the defective product itself must be sought for breach of warranty in contracts rather than in torts.

CHAPTER 3

Misrepresentation

MISREPRESENTATION ROADMAP

- Understand how misrepresentation in torts may be used to circumvent the privity rule in contracts
- Understand the elements of materiality and reliance
- Develop a basic awareness of the practices of social influencers
- Understand the differences between intentional, conscious, negligent, and innocent misrepresentation

---

3.1 Circumventing Privity

Chapter 2 addressed products liability claims that may be brought by those who are given representations about the quality or suitability of a product and are in privity with the defendant. It explained how contract law in many jurisdictions has been prepared to expand beyond the bounds of traditional doctrine to encompass both collateral warranties and an expansive treatment of horizontal privity under section 2-318 of the Uniform Commercial Code (UCC).

Many victims of defective products, nevertheless, have no privity with the defendant, even in states that have adopted that expansive approach. This chapter, therefore, addresses the position of those who are given representations about the quality or suitability of a product but are *not* in privity with the defendant. Since any remedy cannot be sought in contracts, it must instead be sought in the law of torts, specifically the tort of misrepresentation.

Baxter v. Ford Motor Co., 168 Wash. 456, 12 P.2d 409 (1932), illustrates the point. The plaintiff, Baxter, lost his left eye and suffered a loss of sight in his right eye when his car windshield shattered. Ford had provided an express warranty that the windshield would be "shatterproof." If Baxter had bought the car from Ford, he would have had a legitimate claim for breach of an express warranty. But he had not, and since this was before the landmark decision in *Henningsen v. Bloomfield Motors Inc.*, discussed in Chapter 2, this ruled out any claim for breach of warranty because Baxter had no privity of contract with Ford.

Instead, Baxter sued for misrepresentation. The Supreme Court of Washington allowed the claim to proceed because it held that:

> It would be unjust to recognize a rule that would permit manufacturers of goods to create a demand for their products by representing that they possess qualities which they, in fact, do not possess, and then, because there is no privity of contract existing between the consumer and the manufacturer, deny the consumer the right to recover if damages result from the absence of those qualities....

168 Wash. 456, 463 (1932).

Misrepresentation can thus be seen as a means of circumventing the privity rule when a warranty, or something very like it, appears to be provided by a manufacturer. Section 9 of the Third Restatement of Torts: Products Liability puts it this way:

> One engaged in the business of selling or otherwise distributing a product who, in connection with the sale of the product, makes a fraudulent, negligent, or innocent misrepresentation of material fact concerning the product is subject to liability for harm to persons or property caused by the misrepresentation.

A recent example concerns the discovery in 2015 that automobile manufacturer, Volkswagen, had been making a series of demonstrably false marketing claims. Volkswagen had been advertising its diesel vehicles as environmentally friendly, fuel efficient, and high performing. In fact, however, Volkswagen had installed in these cars a defeat device that allowed the vehicles to evade United States Environmental Protection Agency and California Air Resources Board emissions test procedures. The defeat device sensed when a vehicle was undergoing testing and then ensured regulation-compliant results. When driven under normal circumstances, however, the same vehicle would release nitrogen oxides at a factor of up to 40 times over the permitted limit. Over six years, Volkswagen sold American consumers nearly 600,000 diesel vehicles equipped with such a device.

In settling a class action with those buyers for (among other claims) fraudulent misrepresentation, *In re Volkswagen "Clean Diesel" Marketing, Sales Practices, and Products Liability Litigation*, 895 F.3d 597 (2018), Volkswagen agreed to set aside over $10 billion to pay compensation and and other costs.

3.2 Untrue Statements

As section 9 of the Third Restatement of Torts: Products Liability suggests, there are several different types of misrepresentation. But they all require that a false representation was made on which the plaintiff relied.

Just as the typical express warranty requires "an affirmation of fact or promise," a legally actionable misrepresentation originally required reliance on a statement of fact. But, because statements of expert opinion are also likely to be relied upon, they too are now actionable if such reliance was reasonable in all the circumstances of the case.

In *Hanberry v. Hearst*, 276 Cal. App. 2d 680 (1969), for example, Hearst published a monthly magazine, *Good Housekeeping*, in which products were advertised as meeting the "Good Housekeeping's Consumers' Guaranty Seal." The seal promised: "If the product or performance is defective, *Good Housekeeping* guarantees replacement or refund to consumer." The plaintiff bought shoes because the magazine had bestowed its "Seal" upon them. When they proved defective, she brought suit against Hearst.

Hearst's argument that it had merely made a statement of opinion and was, therefore, not actionable received short shrift. California's Fourth District Court of Appeals held that, since the very purpose of the seal was to induce and encourage members of the public to buy the shoes, the defendant was "in poor position to argue its endorsement cannot legally be considered as the inducing factor in bringing about their sale."

3.2.1 Social Media and Celebrity Influencers

Consumers bought *Good Housekeeping* at least partly for its purchase recommendations, because it was seen as an authority whose assessments of product quality could be relied upon. The magazine also made money either from commissions on sales or because manufacturers, whose products were featured, then wanted to advertise in it.

These days, people are less inclined to rely on magazines such as *Good Housekeeping* in deciding which products to buy or use. They instead take their cues from social media or celebrity influencers, many of whom are paid to endorse a specific product. As a result, the Federal Trade Commission (FTC), which is responsible for enforcing the law regarding false advertising, has taken the step of issuing specific guidance for social media influencers, *Guides Concerning the Use of Endorsements and Testimonials in Advertising.* The FTC warns, in particular, that:

> If you endorse a product through social media, your endorsement message should make it obvious when you have a relationship ("material connection") with the brand. A "material connection" to the brand includes a personal, family, or employment relationship or a financial relationship—such as the brand paying you or giving you free or discounted products or services.
>
> Telling your followers about these kinds of relationships is important because it helps keep your recommendations honest and truthful, and it allows people to weigh the value of your endorsements.

Misrepresentation cases against social media influencers have so far been dominated by those giving bad financial advice, but this might be simply because the harm caused has become apparent relatively quickly. Influencers recommending dietary supplements or cosmetics, for example, might be recommending products that cause progressive harm that does not become apparent for some years, so it is possible that this could lead to a number of misrepresentation cases in future.

3.3 Materiality vs Puffery

As the FTC's guidance suggests, any alleged misrepresentation must be "material." In other words, the inaccuracy must have been about a matter on which a reasonable person could be expected to rely.

The clearest instance of when it would be inappropriate to rely on an apparent representation is when that claim constitutes mere puffery. As seen in

Chapter 2, this involves the use of language or images which state or represent something that is:

- Too fanciful to be believed;
- Literally meaningless or impossible; or
- Incapable of verification.

Thus, a claim that a beverage "gives you wings," is not to be taken seriously. Similarly, "If a bubblegum brand advertised that its gum permits chewers to 'blow a bubble as big as the moon,' the statement would be literally false, but it is facially implausible that any reasonable buyer could justifiably rely on that claim." *Int'l Code Council, Inc. v. UpCodes Inc.*, 43 F.4th 46, 60 (2d Cir. 2022).

In *Tietsworth v. Harley Davidson*, 677 N.W.2d 233 (2004), the Supreme Court of Wisconsin held that Harley Davidson's advertising that its motorbikes were of "premium" quality and were "ready to take you thundering down the road" were both examples of puffery because there is no metric by which to judge either claim.

Similarly, claims by Nellie's Free Range Eggs that "We love our hens, you'll love our eggs" or "Better Lives for Hens Mean Better Eggs for You" have been held to be "paradigmatic examples of puffery" because they are "subjective claims about products, which cannot be proven either true or false." By contrast, the claim that "[m]ost hens don't have it as good as Nellie's.... Our hens can peck, perch, and play on plenty of green grass" involved a factual statement upon which a reasonable consumer could rely. *Lugones v. Pete and Gerry's Organic, LLC*, 440 F. Supp. 3d 226, 241 (N.Y. 2020).

Of course, the very fact that salespeople regularly engage in puffery suggests that it is often persuasive. But the fact that some people are persuaded by puffery does not mean that it is reasonable to be persuaded by it. The law will not step in to protect those people from their own foolishness.

On the other hand, when a manufacturer made prominent claims on its packaging that Benecol (a vegetable oil-based spread designed to be used instead of butter) contains "No Trans Fat" and is "Proven to Reduce Cholesterol," the Ninth Circuit held that a reasonable consumer may be entitled to take such claims at face value, even if the presence of partially hydrogenated vegetable oil among the list of ingredients would indicate to a nutritionist that these claims could not be true. *Reid v. Johnson & Johnson*, 780 F.3d 952 (9th Cir. 2015).

3.4 Reliance

If the representation can be shown to be material—i.e., a reasonable person would be likely to rely on it—the plaintiff must then prove that they *did*, in fact, rely on it. Reliance is, essentially, the doctrine through which the plaintiff proves causation of harm in cases of misrepresentation. If the victim did not rely on the statement made by the defendant, it cannot be said that that misrepresentation caused any injury.

In *Stanley v. Wyeth, Inc.*, 991 So. 2d 31 (La. App. 2008), for example, the victim had been prescribed a medication by her doctor. She took the generic form of the medication, but suffered side effects which ultimately led to her death. The court found that, while the drug company had made representations to the medical community, it had never made those representations to the victim. She could not, therefore, have relied upon those representations, and her claim was denied.

Reliance is best shown by establishing that the plaintiff acted differently because of the representation. If that cannot be established, then a court will typically reject the plaintiff's contention of reliance.

The Florida case of *Pop v. Lulifama.com LLC*, Case No. 8:22-cv-2698-VMC-JSS (M.D. Fla. Mar. 20, 2024), illustrates the point. The plaintiff, Pop, had bought what he considered to be defective swimwear after seeing it promoted by social media influencers. The latter had failed to declare that they had been paid for the promotion, and Pop argued that he would never have trusted the promotion if he had known. Yet his claim failed because he failed to articulate any specific statements on which he had relied.

In *Reid v. Johnson & Johnson*, 780 F. 3d 952 (9th Cir. 2015), by contrast, the plaintiff Reid succeeded in showing reliance by saying that he would never have bought Benecol (except, perhaps, at a much reduced price) if it had not been for the heart icon and the misleading claims that it contains "No Trans Fat" and is "Proven to Reduce Cholesterol" on its packaging that suggested it was good for his health.

Of course, not everyone would respond the same way to those claims as Reid did. Someone less concerned about their health would probably have taken little or no notice of the claims made by Benecol's manufacturers. But that does not undermine the fact that *he* had relied on them.

Similarly, in *Campbell v. Whole Foods Market Group, Inc.*, 516 F. Supp. 3d 370 (N.Y. 2021), a consumer was allowed to proceed with her claim of misrepresentation after she bought a packet of honey graham crackers. One of the grounds for her claim was that "graham" flour is a type of whole-wheat flour. Most consumers probably do not realize what "graham" refers to in this context, but the fact that Ms. Campbell was better informed caused her to rely on the representation in a way that the vast majority of other consumers would not have done. In fact, however, the crackers contained significantly more refined flour than whole-wheat flour, and so her claim was legitimate.

3.4.1 Substantial Factor

However, proving reliance on the defendant's misrepresentation does *not* require that the plaintiff prove, on a preponderance of the evidence, that the *only* reason they acted as they did was because of the defendant's misrepresentation. In fact, it is sufficient for the plaintiff to establish that reliance on the defendant's misrepresentation was *one* of the reasons that they acted as they did. *See, e.g., In Re Tobacco II Cases*, 46 Cal. 4th 298, 326 (2009).

In other words, the reliance must have been a "substantial factor" in causing the plaintiff to act as they did. But it is important to emphasize that "substantial" in this context does not mean that reliance on the misrepresentation must have been a "big" reason for the plaintiff's conduct, still less that it must have been the main reason. In this context, "substantial" means that it was a reason "of substance." In other words, it was (a) a genuine reason for the plaintiff's conduct, and (b) not so minimal a factor as to be ignored.

3.4.2 Silence

It might seem odd even to consider whether silence can amount to a statement. Yet the saying "Actions speak louder than words" hints at why it may. If such silence is accompanied by certain behavior, or was preceded by an inaccurate statement, then the failure to speak up or to correct the earlier misstatement may amount to a legally-actionable misrepresentation. When this occurs, it is often known as "concealment" rather than "misrepresentation," but the substance of the tort remains the same.

The law has traditionally been reluctant to impose a positive duty to act or to speak, except in the following three such circumstances:

1. When there is a general legal obligation (e.g., because of a statutory or contractual provision) to do so;

2. When there is a special or fiduciary relationship between the representor and representee; or
3. The representor needs to correct a previous statement which might otherwise be reasonably relied upon by the representee.

3.4.3 General Legal Obligation

An example of an occasion of a general obligation to disclose information is to be found in section 21 C.F.R. § 201.80(e) of the Code of Federal Regulations, which imposes a duty "to include a warning" on manufacturers of prescription drugs and biological products "as soon as there is reasonable evidence of an association of a serious hazard with a drug; a causal relationship need not have been proved."

This is augmented by 73 Fed. Reg. 49605, promulgated by the the Food and Drug Administration (FDA), which requires that:

> Manufacturers continue to have a responsibility under Federal law ... to maintain their labeling and update the labeling with new safety information.

Manufacturers who remain silent in circumstances when these provisions require them proactively to make an appropriate statement will therefore be making a misrepresentation which is potentially just as actionable as if they had actually articulated a misleading statement.

3.4.4 Special or Fiduciary Relationship

A special relationship may be established by "persons who possess unique or specialized expertise, or who are in a special position of confidence and trust with the injured party such that reliance ... is justified." *Kimmell v Schaefer*, 89 N.Y.2d 257, 263 (1996). This means that, in such relationships, one person is effectively taking responsibility for a significant aspect of the other's wellbeing. As a result, the law will not permit the former to remain silent when he or she becomes aware of some information that the other person would likely want to know in order to reach an informed decision in regard to his or her physical safety or financial status.

Thus a physician who is, or becomes, aware of certain potential side-effects of a prescription pharmaceutical is under an obligation to disclose them to a patient before prescribing the drug in question—unless those side-effects are so minor or so unlikely that no reasonable patient could be expected to want to know about them.

It should be emphasized, moreover, that the obligation to proactively disclose information extends beyond the medical field. In *Ponzio v. Mercedes-Benz USA, LLC*, 447 F. Supp. 3d 194, 234 (N.J. 2020), for example, a class action was brought against Mercedes for concealing a problem with a particular paint finish that caused the paint to blister and the car body underneath to corrode. Since Mercedes's knowledge was "exclusive or far superior," a special relationship existed with a customer who had bought her vehicle from a Mercedes dealership. (She was ultimately unsuccessful in her claim, however, because of the economic loss rule, noted in Chapter 2, that prohibits recovery in torts for harm done only to the defective product itself.)

3.4.5 Correcting a Previous Misstatement

It should go without saying that someone who has made an inaccurate statement should, if it is reasonably likely to be relied upon, take appropriate steps to correct the inaccuracy.

This is so even if the previous inaccurate statement was made in good faith. This is to prevent such situations as occurred in *Crocker v. Winthrop Laboratories*, 514 S.W.2d 429 (Tex. 1974). A patient, Crocker, was prescribed a drug called Talwin for pain relief after his doctor had made extensive inquiries to establish that Talwin was non-addictive. Winthrop marketed Talwin as non-addictive because, in their tests and studies submitted to the FDA, addiction had not been recorded as a side-effect. Crocker developed a severe addiction to Talwin, however, and that addiction eventually led to his death. The Supreme Court of Texas held that the manufacturer was liable because although its original representations had been made in good faith, it had failed to correct them when it became aware that they were untrue.

If there were no obligation to correct a previous statement, even though made in good faith at the time, then many patients would be exposed to serious risks which could easily be avoided. The obligation to correct such statements means that other users of Talwin at the time should have been made aware of this risk. The duty to correct a previous misstatement thus encourages the dissemination of new information and keeps the general state of knowledge up to date.

3.5 Fraudulent Misrepresentation

It is now clear that a misrepresentation occurs when a plaintiff can establish either that they reasonably relied on an untrue statement of material fact or expert opinion, or that the defendant failed to disclose information in circumstances where they were under an obligation to do so. The next step is to determine what type of misrepresentation is involved. According to the Second Restatement of Torts, there are four alternatives. In descending order of culpability, they are fraudulent, conscious, negligent, and innocent.

The tort of fraudulent misrepresentation is still sometimes known by its original name in English common law: deceit. Section 557A of the Second Restatement of Torts declares that:

> One who by a fraudulent misrepresentation or nondisclosure of a fact that it is his duty to disclose causes physical harm to the person or to the land or chattel of another who justifiably relies upon the misrepresentation, is subject to liability to the other.

It also provides the following Illustration:

> A, seeking to sell B a shotgun, fraudulently tells B that it is in good condition, although he knows that there is an obstruction in the barrel. B, in reliance on the misrepresentation, buys the gun from A, and discharges it. The gun explodes and B is injured. A is subject to liability to B in an action for deceit.

As this suggests, the tort of fraudulent misrepresentation (or deceit) originally required proof that the defendant intended to mislead. Like several other doctrines already discussed, however, this requirement has been relaxed a little in order to prevent defendants benefiting from "putting their heads in the sand" and arguing that they did not intend the likely consequences. The current methods of proving fraudulent intent are set out in section 526 of the Second Restatement of Torts, though they were, in fact, taken from the nineteenth-century English case of *Derry v. Peek*, [1889] UKHL 1:

> A misrepresentation is fraudulent if the maker
>
> (a) knows or believes the matter is not as he represents it to be,
>
> (b) does not have the confidence in the accuracy of his representation that he states or implies, or
>
> (c) knows that he does not have the basis for his representation that he states or implies.

3.5.1 Pleading with Particularity

These are alternatives; the defendant will be deemed to have acted fraudulently if any one of these tests is applicable. But it is extremely important for a plaintiff to articulate clearly which alternative is alleged, because Rule 9(b) of the Federal Rules of Civil Procedure provides that "[i]n alleging fraud or mistake, a party must state with particularity the circumstances constituting fraud or mistake," although "[m]alice, intent, knowledge, and other conditions of a person's mind may be alleged generally."

The section 526 definition does, however, suffer from a significant omission. It does not address cases of alleged fraudulent *concealment*. In such cases, the plaintiff has to prove that the defendant remained silent because of an intent to deceive. But "[b]y definition," the plaintiffs cannot "point to one particular statement" because concealment involves "a non-statement." *In re Takata Airbag Products Liab. Litig.*, 193 F. Supp. 3d 1324, 1337 (S.D. Fla. 2016). As has been noted in court, *Raymo v. FCA US LLC*, 475 F. Supp. 3d 680, 690 (E.D. Mich. 2020), this means that "fraudulent omissions or concealments are by nature 'more amorphous' than affirmative misrepresentations," so that the pleading standard is "slightly more relaxed." *Baggett v. Hewlett-Packard Co.*, 582 F. Supp. 2d 1261, 1267 (C.D. Cal. 2007).

Because of the high degree of culpability involved in fraudulent misrepresentation, a successful plaintiff is likely to be awarded punitive damages in addition to regular, compensatory damages.

3.5.2 Modifications to the Reliance Requirement

On the other hand, the degree of culpability involved in fraudulent misrepresentation is so high that the plaintiff is not expected to have taken all reasonable steps to avoid being defrauded. As section 545(a) of the Second Restatement of Torts put it: "One who justifiably relies upon a fraudulent misrepresentation is not barred from recovery by his contributory negligence in doing so." In other words, the fraud by the defendant outweighs any negligence by the victim.

On the same basis, section 540 provides that there is no defense to a claim of fraudulent misrepresentation that the victim should have investigated any representation of purported fact, even if "he might have ascertained the falsity of the representation had he made an investigation."

The Restatement takes a different attitude, however, towards representations of expert opinion. Section 542 states:

> The recipient of a fraudulent misrepresentation solely of the maker's opinion is not justified in relying upon it in a transaction with the maker, unless ... the maker
>
> (a) purports to have special knowledge of the matter that the recipient does not have, or
>
> (b) stands in a fiduciary or other similar relation of trust and confidence to the recipient, or
>
> (c) has successfully endeavored to secure the confidence of the recipient, or
>
> (d) has some other special reason to expect that the recipient will rely on his opinion.

3.6 Conscious Misrepresentation

The fact that fraudulent misrepresentation is enumerated within the Second Restatement of Torts as section 557A indicates that it was added after the initial text had been published. Those who later included it saw its original omission as a significant oversight requiring rectification. Yet the original text did include a provision, in section 310, which was arguably intended to cover much the same ground. This it called "conscious" misrepresentation. That occurs when:

> An actor who makes a misrepresentation is subject to liability to another for physical harm which results from an act done by the other or a third person in reliance upon the truth of the representation, if the actor
>
> (a) intends his statement to induce or should realize that it is likely to induce action by the other, or a third person, which involves an unreasonable risk of physical harm to the other, and
>
> (b) knows
>
> (i) that the statement is false, or
>
> (ii) that he has not the knowledge which he professes.

Section 557A is clearly very similar in many respects to section 310, but there are some differences. Section 557A permits a claim not just when the defendant "knows ... that the statement is false" but also when the defendant "knows *or believes* the matter is not as he represents it to be" (emphasis added). It also treats lacking "confidence in the accuracy of [the] state[d] or implie[d]" representation as sufficient to establish the mental element of the tort.

Most significant, however, is the requirement in section 310 that the victim be exposed to "an unreasonable risk of physical harm." There is no equivalent in section 557A. Indeed, this requirement led to Comment (a) to section 557A stating that the liability in section 310 "is *negligence* liability and is enforced in an ordinary negligence action" (emphasis added).

Yet comment (a) to section 9 of the Third Restatement of Torts: Products Liability treats section 310 as dealing with fraudulent misrepresentation! This does seem to have been the original intent of those who drafted section 310. Its requirement to prove "an unreasonable risk of physical harm" seems an unnecessary complication, but it is arguably likely to be met in almost every case.

In practice, most states have tended to recognize *either* section 310 *or* section 557A so far as products liability law is concerned. *Gourdine v. Crews*, 955 A.2d 769 (Md. 2008), for example, treated "conscious" misrepresentation as synonymous with fraud. This would mean that the need to plead with particularity applies to section 310, as would the modifications with respect to reliance.

On the other hand, perhaps the better way to conceptualize the scenario envisioned by section 310 is as a form of gross negligence, enforced by an ordinary negligence action while offering an enhanced likelihood of an award of punitive damages. On that basis, neither the enhanced pleading requirements nor the reliance modifications would apply.

3.7 Negligent Misrepresentation

At the time that *Derry v. Peek* was decided in 1889, the common law recognized only two forms of misrepresentation: fraudulent and non-fraudulent (which, at the time, was often called "innocent misrepresentation"). If the misrepresentation was not fraudulent, then there was only one remedy available, namely rescission of any contract entered into as a result of the misrepresentation. But there was a catch; this required that the contract be with the defendant. If the representation had caused the plaintiff to enter into a contract with a third party, as in *Hanberry v. Hearst*, 276 Cal. App. 2d 680 (1969), they could not rescind that contract.

This often left plaintiffs out of pocket. Indeed, the only financial recompense they could claim was for any payments made according to the terms of the now-rescinded contract. This was called an "indemnity." Any other harm they had suffered as a result of their reliance on the non-fraudulent misrepresentation remained uncompensated.

It became clear that that state of affairs was unfair to many innocent representees. Accordingly, non-fraudulent misrepresentations eventually came to be subdivided into two categories: negligent and innocent. (Note that this means that what is called an "innocent" misrepresentation today is often not identical to what was called an "innocent" misrepresentation in decades past.) Section 311 of the Second Restatement defines negligent misrepresentation as follows:

> (1) One who negligently gives false information to another is subject to liability for physical harm caused by action taken by the other in reasonable reliance upon such information, where such harm results
>
> (a) to the other, or
>
> (b) to such third persons as the actor should expect to be put in peril by the action taken.
>
> (2) Such negligence may consist of failure to exercise reasonable care
>
> (a) in ascertaining the accuracy of the information, or
>
> (b) in the manner in which it is communicated.

As the Supreme Court of Mississippi once put it, *First Money, Inc. v. Frisby*, 369 So. 2d 746, 750 (Miss. 1979): "The basis for damages resulting from negligent misrepresentation is the lack of care; the basis for damages resulting from fraud is the want of honesty." Since the level of wrongdoing to be proved here is that of negligence, it is perfectly proper for the defendant to allege the plaintiff's own contributory negligence or comparative fault as a full or partial defense.

Nevertheless, even if the circumstances of a particular case might seem to warrant a claim of fraudulent misrepresentation, it will still usually be good practice for a plaintiff to plead negligent misrepresentation in the alternative. Not only will this provide a sort of "second-best" option for the plaintiff if they turn out to be unable to sustain the claim of fraudulent misrepresentation, but the type of evidence that the plaintiff is likely to need in the attempt to prove fraudulent misrepresentation is also likely to be germane to any attempt to prove gross negligence (thus paving the way for an award of punitive damages even without the plaintiff's proving that the defendant acted fraudulently).

In *Wallace v. ConAgra Foods, Inc.*, 747 F.3d 1025, 1027, 1028 (8th Cir. 2014), the Eighth Circuit addressed multiple claims of misrepresentation that had been brought on the basis that "some Hebrew National beef products are not, as the label reads, '100% kosher.'"

> According to the consumers, manufacturing quotas—not kosher rules—are the deciding factor as to whether any batch of meat harvested at the ... slaughterhouses is ultimately designated as kosher or non-kosher. Employees face such pressure to meet a quota of approximately 70% for kosher meat that "the kosher inspection process becomes defective and unreliable" and some "meat from cows that should not qualify for kosher certification ends up being marked kosher and used in Hebrew National products."

Interestingly, the plaintiffs did not purchase or consume Hebrew National brand products for reasons of faith, but instead claimed to rely on the manufacturer's representations that:

> [K]osher is the "New Organic," a promise of food purity amid other products full of artificial ingredients, [which] led them to pay an unjustified premium for Hebrew National's ostensibly kosher beef.

In other words, the loss they claimed was neither religious nor physical—they had not become ill after eating Hebrew National beef—but economic. The court agreed. In the end, however, it denied all the claims because, even if the plaintiffs' allegations were true, they could not establish that "that any of the particular packages of Hebrew National beef they personally purchased contained non-kosher beef." It was not persuaded by the plaintiffs' argument that "it is impossible for any reasonable consumer to detect" whether purportedly kosher meat is non-kosher:

> [I]t is pure speculation to say the particular packages sold to the consumers were tainted by non-kosher beef, while it is quite plausible [the defendants] sold the consumers exactly what was promised: a higher quality, kosher meat product.

Wallace v. ConAgra Foods, Inc., 747 F.3d 1025, 1030, 1031 (8th Cir. 2014).

3.8 Innocent Misrepresentation

The last form of misrepresentation recognized by the courts is that of innocent misrepresentation. As its name suggests, it applies even though the defendant was not at fault. *Crocker v. Winthrop Laboratories*, noted above, illustrates the point. The pharmaceutical manufacturer was held liable for the harm caused by its drug, Talwin, that it had marketed with the specific representation that it was free and safe from all dangers of addiction. This representation rested on reasonable grounds because no addiction had been recorded in the company's testing. Nevertheless, "when the treating physician relies upon that representation, the drug company is liable when the representation proves to be false and harm results." 514 S.W.2d 429, 433 (Tex. 1974).

It is normally inadvisable, however, for a plaintiff to bring suit for innocent misrepresentation alone. For one thing, such a case will be defeated by evidence of comparative fault, if the plaintiff was at greater fault than the defendant. Secondly, even if a case of innocent misrepresentation is proved, punitive damages will never be awarded because the defendant was not at fault, and so there is no justification for punishment. Thirdly, since it involves no fault, a claim for breach of warranty (which also does not require proof of fault) will almost always be more attractive.

Moreover, while it may be brought alongside other theories of products liability, the plaintiff runs a tactical risk in doing so because it may undermine those other theories to suggest that the defendant was not at fault. In truth, claims of actionable, innocent misrepresentations which do not involve other torts or a breach of warranty are rare. For all these reasons, claims of innocent misrepresentation are not commonly alleged.

MISREPRESENTATION CHECKPOINTS

- Misrepresentations involve an untrue statement of fact or expert opinion.
- They must be material and not puffery.
- They must be relied upon by the plaintiff, even if others would respond differently.
- Concealment is a form of misrepresentation if there was a duty to disclose a material fact.

- A duty to disclose may arise:
  - from a general legal obligation;
  - from a special or fiduciary duty; or
  - out of a need to correct a previous statement (even if that had been made with good faith at the time).
- Misrepresentations may be:
  - fraudulent;
  - conscious;
  - negligent; or
  - innocent.
- Fraudulent misrepresentation must be pleaded with particularity, but the reliance requirements may be relaxed if the misstatement was one of purported fact.

CHAPTER 4

Negligence

NEGLIGENCE ROADMAP

- Understand the state of the common law in the nineteenth century
- Understand the elements of negligence
- Understand the difference between questions of law for the judge and questions of fact for the jury
- Understand *res ipsa loquitur*, the role of inference, and the different approaches of the Second and Third Restatements of Torts

---

4.1 Summary of the Original Common Law

Previous chapters have outlined how nineteenth-century common law initially held product sellers liable for harm caused by their defective products only if (a) the victim and seller were in privity of contract and (b) there had been a breach of an express warranty. It slowly relaxed that position, so that by the end of the century, most jurisdictions also recognized claims for (a) breaches of statutorily-imposed implied warranties and (b) misrepresentations in torts. For the latter, privity was not required. By the early twentieth century, therefore, a victim had four potential avenues through which to bring a claim, namely:

- Breach of express warranty;
- Breach of implied warranty;

- Fraudulent misrepresentation (deceit); and
- Non-fraudulent (typically called innocent) misrepresentation.

While this development clearly provided more protection for users and consumers of products than had been provided in the nineteenth century, it still left the vast majority of victims of defective products without any means of redress. In particular, a victim who did not have privity and who was not the victim of a fraudulent misrepresentation would essentially be out of luck. Even if they had been the victim of an innocent misrepresentation, the remedies available for that were (as explained in Chapter 3) barely worth the candle. And if there had been no misrepresentation at all, then even that small crumb of comfort was denied.

Even though its kingdom had contracted a little, *caveat emptor* still reigned supreme. Unless the victim could bring their case within one of these theories, then the courts would deny liability.

4.2 Duty of Care to Users

In 1916 Judge Benjamin Cardozo of the New York Court of Appeals forever changed that legal landscape. In *MacPherson v. Buick Motor Co.*, 217 N.Y. 382 (1916), Buick had made and sold a car to a retail dealership, which then resold it to MacPherson. While MacPherson was in the car, it suddenly collapsed as the spokes of one of the wheels "crumbled into fragments." He was thrown out and injured. It turned out that the spokes had been made from defective wood.

MacPherson had clearly not been in privity of contract with Buick, and the idea of his having a collateral contract with Buick that ran alongside the main contract of sale with the dealership (see Chapter 2) had not yet been recognized. Moreover, MacPherson had not been the victim of a misrepresentation. On the basis of the common law at the time, he should have been denied compensation. But Cardozo did not agree:

> If the nature of a thing is such that it is reasonably certain to place life and limb in peril when negligently made, it is then a thing of danger. Its nature gives warning of the consequences to be expected. If to the element of danger there is added knowledge that the thing will be used by persons other than the purchaser, and used without new tests then,

> irrespective of contract, the manufacturer of this thing of danger is under a duty to make it carefully.

The modern law of products liability was born. It was not fully fledged, of course. In fact, it would be almost another 40 years before it could be said to have come of age. But *MacPherson* changed the legal landscape forever.

Manufacturers could no longer simply look to, in the words of British entrepreneur Sir Jack Cohen, "pile it high and sell it cheap." They now also had to take care to make products safe. How much care was not stated. The point was that manufacturers now had a new legal duty. As Cardozo explained, 217 N.Y. 382, 393 (1916):

> There is nothing anomalous in a rule which imposes upon A, who has contracted with B, a duty to C and D and others according as he knows or does not know that the subject matter of the contract is intended for their use.

Most importantly, he emphasized, 217 N.Y. 382, 390 (1916), that the source of this duty was in torts and not in contracts:

> We have put aside the notion that the duty to safeguard life and limb, when the consequences of negligence may be foreseen, grows out of contract and nothing else. We have put the source of the obligation where it ought to be. We have put its source in the law.

Cardozo's approach has since been memorialized in section 395 of the Second Restatement of Torts:

> A manufacturer who fails to exercise reasonable care in the manufacture of a chattel which, unless carefully made, he should recognize as involving an unreasonable risk of causing physical harm to those who use it for a purpose for which the manufacturer should expect it to be used and to those whom he should expect to be endangered by its probable use, is subject to liability for physical harm caused to them by its lawful use in a manner and for a purpose for which it is supplied.

It is important to note that neither *MacPherson* nor section 395 impose an open-ended duty on a manufacturer towards the whole world. Anyone injured by a defective product must have been reasonably foreseeable to interact with that product. They need not be the owner of the product in question; a passenger in a car or an employee using a product supplied by their employer would certainly qualify. But a random bystander would not.

4.3 Duty vs Standard of Care

Duty of care and standard of care are often confused, but they actually relate to very different facets of a case. Duty is concerned with *whether* the defendant owed the plaintiff any sort of obligation in the law of torts. If such a duty is established, then standard of care is the doctrine that addresses what quality or level of care was required.

This distinction is not just of analytical significance; it also has major practical implications. Whereas the question of whether a duty is owed is a matter of law for the court (as in *MacPherson* itself), the issue of the appropriate standard of care is typically a matter decided by a jury according to the facts of the case. The one exception to the latter statement occurs when the evidence can only support one side's argument. If that happens, the judge will then decide the question of standard of care as a matter of law.

Because duty is *always* a matter of law, it is the one element of an alleged case of negligence that lends itself easily to summary judgment. For this reason, defendants typically argue that an alleged case of negligence against them should be dismissed on the grounds that the plaintiff has failed to establish a duty. If that plea is successful, a case pled in negligence will fail. (Other theories of the case alleged by the plaintiff might, of course, still be valid.) On the other hand, if the judge rules that the defendant *did* owe the plaintiff a duty of care, the defendant may well choose to try to negotiate a settlement rather than risk an unpredictable verdict from the jury.

4.4 Standard of Care and Breach of Duty

If a duty is held to exist, and the jury has then determined the appropriate standard of care, it must then consider whether the defendant lived up to that standard. A breach of duty has occurred if the jury finds that the appropriate standard of care was not met. From the plaintiff's point of view, this means that they must first seek to establish what the defendant should have done, and then go on to show that the defendant did not, in fact, behave in such a manner.

If the defendant is in breach of duty, then they are at fault. It clearly does not involve the same egregious degree of fault as fraud, and so punitive damages tend to be awarded in only around 5% of cases where negligence is proved. But it is fault nonetheless, because it means that the defendant could and should have done better.

Juries are not constrained by what previous juries have decided, and they are typically comprised of novices who have never served on a jury before. This does not mean, however, that they are free to make wholly arbitrary decisions. The law has put guardrails in place to narrow the scope of jury decision-making.

The first of those guardrails is that the judge will step in to decide as a matter of law the questions of either standard of care or breach of duty (or both) if the evidence relevant to one or other doctrine supports the case only of the plaintiff or only of the defendant. It follows, therefore, that if the judge does not do so, a verdict for either party is capable of being supported by the evidence presented.

Secondly, the jury is told that the standard of care expected of the defendant is "reasonableness." In other words, the jury is tasked with answering the question of whether the defendant behaved reasonably. Section 291 of the Second Restatement of Torts attempts to explain the position thus:

> Where an act is one which a reasonable man would recognize as involving a risk of harm to another, the risk is unreasonable and the act is negligent if the risk is of such magnitude as to outweigh what the law regards as the utility of the act or of the particular manner in which it is done.

This is, however, a little misleading in that "the law" does not actually have a fixed standard. It is for the jury to work out what reasonableness means. It certainly is not limited to a purely economic calculation of weighing harm and utility. Like the Declaration of Independence, it embraces the original utilitarian appeal to what John Stuart Mill called "the greatest amount of happiness altogether." Thus the test of unreasonableness is better viewed as asking the jury whether the act done was likely to increase or decrease the sum total of human happiness.

4.5 A Duty to Innovate?

In the *Gilead Tenofovir Cases*, 98 Cal. App. 5th 911, 927 (2024), the First District Court of Appeals of California observed that, "although the utility of a cause of action for negligence in products liability actions has been greatly reduced by the doctrine of strict liability, it has not been eliminated."

The relevant facts were that defendant Gilead developed and sold one of the first medications to treat HIV/AIDS. That drug, tenofovir disoproxil fumarate (TDF), was approved for sale by the Food and Drug Administration (FDA) in 2001. Although TDF was effective in suppressing the effects of HIV, its use carried a risk of skeletal and kidney damage. The 24,000 plaintiffs in these cases alleged that they had suffered these or other adverse effects from their use of TDF.

While Gilead was developing TDF, it discovered a similar but chemically distinct compound, tenofovir alafenamide fumarate (TAF). The plaintiffs alleged that Gilead's early testing indicated TAF could be as effective as TDF at treating HIV/AIDS, while carrying a lower risk of adverse effects, but that Gilead chose to defer development of TAF because it was concerned that immediate development of TAF would cannibalize its profits from TDF. Years later, Gilead resumed the development of TAF and obtained FDA approval for its sale in 2015.

On this basis, the plaintiffs argued that Gilead's decision to defer development of TAF to maximize its profits breached its duty of reasonable care to users of TDF. Both the trial and appellate court allowed that claim to proceed, though the latter dismissed the plaintiff's alternative claim of fraudulent concealment.

Critics of this decision have opined that the court effectively imposed on manufacturers a novel duty to innovate. The court itself rejected that criticism, noting that negligence can take many forms, not all of which require proof of a defective product. It will be interesting to see which approach is favored by the Supreme Court of California, which has agreed to review the case.

4.6 *Res Ipsa Loquitur* and the Fault Requirement

It is now clear that the plaintiff in a negligence action must prove, on a preponderance of the evidence, (a) that they were owed a duty of care by the defendant, and (b) that the duty was breached because the defendant failed to meet the expected standard of care of reasonable conduct. There are times, however, when establishing the latter requirement may be virtually impossible because the plaintiff simply lacks the relevant information to be able to prove the point. Nor will pre-trial orders of discovery of documents always help for, if there are no relevant documents in existence, there will be nothing to discover.

The California case of *Escola v. Coca Cola Bottling Co.*, 24 Cal. 2d 453, 456, 457 (1944), provides a helpful example. In *Escola*, a waitress in a restaurant was injured when a bottle of Coca Cola broke in her hand, apparently because of "excessive pressure of gas or by reason of some defect in the bottle." Giving the judgment of the court, Chief Justice Gibson affirmed judgment for the plaintiff by permitting the use of inference to establish the defendant's fault:

> Plaintiff then rested her case, having announced to the court that being unable to show any specific acts of negligence she relied completely on the doctrine of *res ipsa loquitur*.

The phrase *res ipsa loquitur* means "the thing speaks for itself." He continued, 24 Cal. 2d 453, 461 (1944):

> Although it is not clear in this case whether the explosion was caused by an excessive charge or a defect in the glass, there is a sufficient showing that neither cause would ordinarily have been present if due care had been used. Further, defendant had exclusive control over both the charging and inspection of the bottles. Accordingly, all the requirements necessary to entitle plaintiff to rely on the doctrine of *res ipsa loquitur* to supply an inference of negligence are present.

In other words, in the circumstances of the case, it was perfectly acceptable to draw the inference that the glass broke because of the defendant's lack of care.

It is important to appreciate that application of *res ipsa loquitur* does not transform the tort of negligence into one of strict liability in a manner analogous to cases of breach of warranty in contracts. Even when applying *res ipsa loquitur*, the law remains focused on whether the defendant has behaved unreasonably. The doctrine's significance lies in the fact that *it permits, but does not require*, the fact-finder to draw inferences of the defendant's negligence from known, primary facts in circumstances where it is difficult to explain how the plaintiff could have been injured otherwise.

Section 328D(1) of the Second Restatement of Torts generalized from *Escola* to indicate when *res ipsa loquitur* may legitimately be pleaded:

> (a) the event is of a kind which ordinarily does not occur in the absence of negligence;
>
> (b) other responsible causes, including the conduct of the plaintiff and third persons, are sufficiently eliminated by the evidence; and
>
> (c) the indicated negligence is within the scope of defendant's duty to the plaintiff.

It is, however, unfortunate that subsection (a) speaks of "negligence," since that might be taken to imply that *res ipsa loquitur* may be pleaded in order to avoid having to establish any element of the tort of negligence. That is not what is meant here. In fact, "negligence" in this context is used as a synonym for "unreasonableness."

Section 328D(2) and (3) together make it clear that it is for the judge to decide whether these circumstances exist so that the plea may legitimately be made. If the plea is permitted, it is then for the jury to determine whether the inference that the plaintiff claims should be drawn. That is, unless the judge takes the view that the inference *must* be drawn, in which case they should so rule as a matter of law.

4.6.1 Second vs Third Restatement

The Third Restatement of Torts: Physical and Emotional Harm has, however, removed the need for requirement (b). Instead, section 17 permits "the factfinder [to] infer that the defendant has been negligent when the accident" was *one of* the causes of the plaintiff's harm. This brings the application of *res ipsa loquitur* onto the same footing as the rest of the doctrine of causation, which fully recognizes that an injury may have more than one cause.

In *Rizzo v. Corning, Inc.*, 105 F. 3d 338, 340 (1997), for example, the Seventh Circuit affirmed judgment for the plaintiff in a case where he had been badly burned after the coffee carafe he was holding had suddenly broken in two:

> [A]t the exact moment when the carafe, in its journey toward his wife's cup, was directly over his lap, it broke in two, spilling the coffee (which was heated to between 170 and 180 degrees Fahrenheit) into Mr. Rizzo's lap and causing second-degree burns....
>
> The plaintiffs tried to prove their case by two alternative routes. The first, and thoroughly conventional, was to show that the carafe had in fact a specific, demonstrable manufacturing defect.... Alternatively, they relied on a form or variant of *res ipsa loquitur* [where] the jury is allowed to infer, despite the absence of evidence of a specific defect, that the accident was indeed the result of a product defect for which the manufacturer is liable....
>
> In these unusual circumstances the accident itself is sufficient evidence of a defect to permit, though of course not compel, the jury to infer a defect. Whether these were the circumstances of the accident was a jury question. The jury was not, as the defendants argue, required to disregard the Rizzos' testimony that they didn't bang the carafe against the wall or otherwise abuse it, merely because the testimony was self-serving. Self-serving it was; but the testimony of the defendants' expert, an employee of one of the defendants, could be considered equally self-serving.

Nevertheless, not every jurisdiction has adopted the Third Restatement approach; some still prefer that of the Second Restatement. In Georgia, for example, the decision rendered by the Court of Appeals of Georgia, *U.S. Fidelity & Co. v. J.I. Case Co.*, 209 Ga. App. 61, 64–65 (1993), before publication of the Third Restatement, is still treated as an authoritative statement of the law:

> The principal basis for application of the rule of *res ipsa loquitur* is that the occurrence involved would not have occurred but for negligence, and this negligence may properly be charged to the person in *exclusive* control of the instrumentality. (Emphasis added.)

In Indiana, too, proof of exclusive management and control is still required. In *Griffin v. Menard, Inc.*, for example, a shopper found a sink he liked in a store and grabbed the box from the shelf. But the box's staples were loose, so the bottom of the box came open and the sink fell on him. He sued the store, who joined the manufacturer of the sink as a co-defendant. The court held, 175 N.E.3d 811, 816 (Ind. 2021), that "it seems like speculation that the only way the sink could have fallen out of the box was because [the defendant] was negligent when the box could have been handled/tampered with by another customer." Accordingly, it declined to apply *res ipsa loquitur* in the plaintiff's favor.

4.6.2 Food vs Other Products

Cases involving allegedly defective food have, however, always seen the courts impose higher standards on defendants. In *Matthews v. Yoplait USA, Inc.*, 835 S.E.2d 393 (Ga. 2019), for example, a woman had 17 metal fragments, measuring over 1.5mm in size, surgically removed from her gastrointestinal tract after a eating a mouthful or two of strawberry yoghurt.

This time, the Georgia Court of Appeals took the view that whether *res ipsa loquitur* applied was a matter of fact for the jury to determine. The doctrine could not be ruled inapplicable merely because the defendant, Yoplait, offered evidence that it scanned its yoghurt prior to sealing its containers. There was, after all, evidence that such scanning took place only before the adding of fruit, while its quality control manager had testified, 835 S.E. 2d 393, 395 (Ga. 2019), that although she had "very rarely" seen metal in yogurt, it was "not unheard of."

The court held, 835 S.E.2d 393, 396–97 (Ga. 2019):

> If the evidence includes an incomplete explanation of the facts of the occurrence to the extent that the true cause is still left in doubt or is not clearly shown, the doctrine of *res ipsa loquitur* remains in the case, leaving to the jury a permissible inference of negligence for them to accept or reject.

The court cited with approval its own prior case of *Persinger v. Step By Step Infant Dev. Center* where it had held, 560 S.E.2d 333, 337 (Ga. 2002), that "*res ipsa loquitur* does not require elimination of all other possible occurrences; it must only 'render less probable all inconsistent conclusions.'"

Similarly, the Indiana Court of Appeals ruled in *Golden Corral Corp. v. Lenart* that a jury was correctly allowed to decide that *res ipsa loquitur* applied in a case where the plaintiff had become ill and been treated overnight in an emergency room after eating chicken wings at a Golden Corral buffet. Clearly, the food in the buffet "could have been handled/tampered with by another customer." Yet the court, 127 N.E.3d 1205, 1219 (Ind. 2019), took a different tack here: "It is not necessary for a plaintiff to exclude every other possibility other than the defendant's negligence as a cause for the plaintiff's injury."

4.7 Negligence Per Se

Sometimes the law goes further than permitting the fact-finder—normally the jury—to draw inferences from known primary facts. It may instead, as section 874A of the Second Restatement of Torts recognizes, mandate a finding of breach of duty in negligence as a matter of law because of a breach of a legislative or regulatory requirement laid down by criminal or administrative law. This is known as "negligence *per se*": negligence in and of itself.

The idea of negligence *per se* is controversial in a number of respects. One is that it involves creating a rule of torts out of a provision originally found in criminal or administrative law. It is not a matter of the legislature or regulatory agency expressly attempting to create a new form of tort. Quite the reverse: the point of negligence *per se* is that it involves the courts developing a rule for torts where the original criminal or legislative provision was silent. As section 285(b) of the Restatement (Second) of Torts (1965) puts it:

> The standard of conduct of a reasonable man may be ... adopted by the court from a legislative enactment or an administrative regulation which does not so provide.

This is made possible by answering yes to each of four questions, the first two of which are as follows:

1. Was the plaintiff in the instant case a member of the class of persons whom the original provision was designed to protect?
2. Was the harm suffered by the plaintiff of the type that the original provision was designed to prevent or deter?

The case of *Stanton by Brooks v. Astra Pharmaceutical Products, Inc.* provides a tragic example. Harrikah Stanton, an eight-month-old infant, had a bone-marrow test in December 1971 to determine the cause of the hemolytic anemia from which she had suffered since birth. In performing the test, the hematologist injected a two-percent solution of Xylocaine into Harrikah's right posterior iliac crest to anesthetize the area from which he would aspirate bone marrow. Shortly after the procedure, Harrikah began convulsing and experienced cardiac and respiratory arrest. Attempts to resuscitate her had little effect. The cardiac arrest resulted in severe and irreversible brain damage, so that she was rendered unable to walk, talk, or stand and required constant care for the rest of her life. It subsequently became apparent that Astra, the manufacturer of Xylocaine, had failed to file with the Food and Drug Administration (the "FDA") certain reports about the drug, as required by federal statutes and regulations. The Third Circuit ruled, 718 F. 2d 553, 563 (1983):

> Under Pennsylvania law, the violation of a governmental safety regulation constitutes negligence per se if the regulation "was, in part, intended to protect the interest of another as an individual [and] the interest of the plaintiff which was invaded ... was one which the act intended to protect." Astra cannot seriously dispute that [the law] was promulgated to protect individuals such as Harrikah Stanton from precisely the type of harm that here occurred—an unexpected adverse reaction to Xylocaine. It thus would appear that Astra's failure to file the reports constituted negligence per se.

Section 14 of the Restatement (Third) of Torts: Liability for Physical and Emotional Harm attempts to re-state the law succinctly by including *only* the two questions noted above. Nevertheless, positive answers to both of these questions are insufficient to establish negligence *per se*. A third question must also be addressed, as follows:

3. Would the policy behind the original provision be appropriately served by using it to impose civil liability?

This raises a question of law, which requires the court to infer the policy behind the original criminal or administrative provision, and then decide whether that policy is furthered or hindered by the development of a new rule in torts. As was said in *Frederick L. v. Thomas*, 578 F.2d 513, 516–17 (3d Cir. 1978), "an incorrect interpretation of state law might arguably interfere with important state policies," so it is important for a court to ensure that any new rule cannot "affront the Legislature's declared intent." *Gorton v. J.W. Mashburn*, 995 P.2d 1114, 1117 (Okla. 1999).

Federalism highlights the significance of this question. As tort law is a matter for the states, the question arises whether it can be appropriate to invoke negligence *per se* if the original criminal or administrative provision stems from federal law. As the Sixth Circuit commented in *In re Bendectin Litigation*, 857 F.2d 290, 313 (1988):

> [T]he determination that a violation of a federal statute such as the FDCA will create state tort liability is not a matter solely of state law. A state's ability to use a federal statute violation as a basis for state tort

liability and negligence per se depends on the intent of Congress, and not merely on the intent of the state. Thus, the congressional decision not to provide a private cause of action under the FDCA becomes quite important in considering the propriety of a state negligence per se action for violation of the FDCA.

Finally, the fourth question is this:

4. Is it possible to make the rule sufficiently precise?

A standard that is vague or confused cannot form the basis of negligence *per se* because it would be unfair to impose liability on a defendant when they had no opportunity to know in advance what they are expected to do. As the Fifth Circuit explained in *Dougherty v. Santa Fe Marine, Inc.*, 698 F.2d 232, 235 (1983):

> Implicit in virtually all discussions of negligence per se is the unspoken assumption that the regulation in question establishes a clear minimum standard of care. If the regulation fails to do so, the reason for applying the doctrine fades. An ambiguous or contradictory regulatory standard defeats the certainty on which the rule of per se liability rests. Persons affected are deprived of a sure standard upon which they may fashion their affairs.

NEGLIGENCE CHECKPOINTS

- Negligence requires proof of both a duty of care and a breach of that duty.
- Duty is a question of law for the court; breach is a question of fact for the jury.
- *Res ipsa loquitur* may be available to allow a jury to infer a breach of duty if:
    - the event is of a kind which ordinarily does not occur in the absence of negligence; and
    - the indicated negligence is within the scope of defendant's duty to the plaintiff.

- Some jurisdictions also require that other responsible causes, including the conduct of the plaintiff and third persons, are sufficiently eliminated by the evidence in order to enable a plea of *res ipsa loquitur*.
- Negligence *per se* may also be used to establish a breach of duty if all the following questions are answered in the affirmative:
    - Was the plaintiff in the instant case a member of the class of persons whom the original provision was designed to protect?
    - Was the harm suffered by the plaintiff of the type that the original provision was designed to prevent or deter?
    - Would the policy behind the original provision be appropriately served by using it to impose civil liability?
    - Is it possible to make the rule sufficiently precise?

CHAPTER 5

Second vs Third Restatements

SECOND VS THIRD RESTATEMENTS ROADMAP

- Understand the state of the law in the mid-twentieth century
- Understand the practical ramifications of bringing an action in contracts versus torts
- Understand Justice Roger Traynor's arguments for strict liability in torts
- Understand the differences between the approaches of the Second and Third Restatements

---

5.1 Contracts vs Torts Revisited (Again)

As Chapter 4 explained, the law regulating liability for defective products had, by the mid-twentieth century, grown from being concerned only with false statements of purported fact or expert opinion to include negligence as well. By the middle of the twentieth century, therefore, a victim had six potential avenues through which to bring a claim, namely:

- Breach of express warranty;
- Breach of implied warranty;
- Fraudulent misrepresentation (deceit);
- Negligent misrepresentation;
- Innocent misrepresentation; and
- Negligence.

As has already been noted, each of these theories requires different elements to be proved. But one difference transcended all others. Breaches of warranty were actions to be brought in contracts, while all the others were actions that lay in torts.

The implications of that difference are worth repeating. They are:

- Actions in contracts require proof of some sort of privity, whereas actions in torts do not.
- Compensation for harm done to the defective product itself is available for actions in contracts but, because of the economic loss rule, never in torts.
- Punitive damages may be available for actions in torts (especially deceit), but are never available in contracts.
- Actions in torts typically require proof of fault, whereas those in contracts do not.

5.2 Fault vs Strict Liability Revisited

As the twentieth century moved towards its second half, however, the courts began to question whether the last of these differences remained justifiable. The first significant doubt was uttered by Justice Roger Traynor of the California Supreme Court in *Escola v. Coca Cola Bottling Co.*, 24 Cal. 2d 453, 462 (1944):

> Even if there is no negligence, ... public policy demands that responsibility be fixed wherever it will most effectively reduce the hazards to life and health inherent in defective products that reach the market.

As explained in Chapter 4, Traynor's argument was *not* the basis of the court's decision in *Escola*; in fact, that rested on *res ipsa loquitur*. But Traynor wanted to take things further and impose strict liability—i.e., liability without fault—on product distributors *in torts*. This was a striking new argument.

Traynor justified his position in two ways. First, with the development of mass-produced products, he considered this to be an issue of public health and safety. Those in charge of bringing potentially dangerous products to market should, therefore, be strongly encouraged to take great care to ensure that their products are safe. Secondly, there are likely to be many cases where a defective product injures someone, and yet all the parties—victim, manufacturer, and distributor—are blameless. In such cases, he argued, it makes the most sense to have the cost of such harm borne by the party in the best position to bear it. As Traynor himself said, 24 Cal. 2d 453, 462–63 (1944):

> It is evident that the manufacturer can anticipate some hazards and guard against the recurrence of others, as the public cannot. Those who suffer injury from defective products are unprepared to meet its consequences. The cost of an injury and the loss of time or health may be an overwhelming misfortune to the person injured, and a needless one, for the risk of injury can be insured by the manufacturer and distributed among the public as a cost of doing business.... Against such a risk there should be general and constant protection and the manufacturer is best situated to afford such protection.... If public policy demands that a manufacturer of goods be responsible for their quality regardless of negligence there is no reason not to fix that responsibility openly.

5.3 Change of Focus

Arguably just as important as the change in the substantive law for which Traynor was arguing was the change in rhetorical focus that it implied. For Traynor, the focus should be not on what the defendant did, but on whether the product was defective or not.

If a product was defective and that defect caused harm, then the defendant should be liable. The nature of the defendant's conduct was, for him, immaterial. After all, it was their product that had proved defective and caused harm; there should be no need for the plaintiff to prove anything else. This would not mean open-ended liability. As Traynor himself pointed out, 24 Cal. 2d 453, 468 (1944), in *Escola*:

> The manufacturer's liability should, of course, be defined in terms of the safety of the product in normal and proper use, and should not extend to injuries that cannot be traced to the product as it reached the market.

In other words, Traynor sought to make manufacturers and distributors strictly liable for products that were not of merchantable quality. But he sought to do this not just in contracts through claims for breach of warranty but also in torts.

The significance of this approach lay in its abandoning any need to establish privity between the plaintiff and defendant in order to pursue a strict liability claim.

Twenty years after *Escola*, Justice Traynor's idea of no-fault products liability in torts finally became orthodoxy in California when the state's Supreme Court decided *Greenman v. Yuba Power Products, Inc.* In that case, a wife bought her husband a Shopsmith power tool as a Christmas present. A year later he bought the necessary attachments to use the Shopsmith as a lathe. After working on a piece of wood several times without difficulty, it "suddenly flew out of the machine and struck him on the forehead, inflicting serious injuries." 59 Cal. 2d 57, 57 (1963).

The plaintiff's experts testified that the screws used to hold parts of the machine together were inadequate, so that normal vibration caused it to become loose. Writing for the Court, Justice Traynor declared, 59 Cal. 2d 57, 62–63 (1963):

> [T]o impose strict liability on the manufacturer under the circumstances of this case, it was not necessary for plaintiff to establish an express warranty.... A manufacturer is strictly liable in tort when an article he places on the market, knowing that it is to be used without inspection for defects, proves to have a defect that causes injury to a human being.... Although ... strict liability has usually been based on the theory of an express or implied warranty running from the manufacturer to the plaintiff, ... the liability is not one governed by the law of contract warranties but by the law of strict liability in tort.

Greenman marked a new departure for the law of torts in products liability cases. While there had always been a stricter approach to cases involving food, other allegedly defective products could, until *Greenman*, provide a basis for liability only if the defendant could be shown to have been negligent along the lines that Chief Judge Cardozo had explained fifty years earlier in *MacPherson v. Buick Motor Co.*, 217 N.Y. 382 (1916). *Greenman* effectively left Cardozo's duty requirement intact, but dispensed with any need for the plaintiff to prove a breach of that duty.

It is hard to overstate the significance of *Greenman*. The following year, in *Vandermark v. Ford Motor Co.*, 61 Cal. 2d 256 (1964), Traynor—again giving the judgment of a unanimous California Supreme Court—extended such liability beyond manufacturers to include retailers. In 1996, the Association of Trial Lawyers of America celebrated its 50th anniversary by asking tort lawyers and law professors to nominate their top ten developments in tort law during the Association's existence. *Greenman* headed the list.

5.4 The Second Restatement

Greenman soon came to be accepted as the authoritative statement of products liability law in several states outside California. Accordingly, the American Law Institute (ALI) deemed it necessary to add a new section to the Second Restatement of Torts to reflect this new development. Section 402A(1) reads:

> One who sells any product in a defective condition unreasonably dangerous to the user or consumer or to his property is subject to liability for physical harm thereby caused to the ultimate user or consumer, or to his property, if
>
> (a) the seller is engaged in the business of selling such a product, and
>
> (b) it is expected to and does reach the user or consumer without substantial change in the condition in which it is sold.

Unfortunately, this wording did not so much clarify the law as sow seeds of confusion. While most of it is unexceptionable, the phrase "unreasonably dangerous" has been the source of much controversy. The whole point of Traynor's approach in *Escola* and *Greenman* had been to move away from the need to prove unreasonable conduct on the part of the defendant in favor of strict liability. Yet section 402A(1) still talked of unreasonableness, albeit this time applied to the danger created by the product rather than the defendant's conduct.

Some states that otherwise continue to follow the Second Restatement simply do not recognize any need to prove that a defective product is unreasonably dangerous. Other commentators have argued that the phrase "unreasonably dangerous" is designed simply to explain what makes a product defective. For example, the section's author, Professor Prosser, explained in Comment *i* that:

> Many products cannot possibly be made entirely safe for all consumption, and any food or drug necessarily involves some risk of harm, if only from over-consumption. Ordinary sugar is a deadly poison to diabetics, and castor oil found use under Mussolini as an instrument of torture. That is not what is meant by unreasonably dangerous in this Section. The article sold must be dangerous to an extent beyond that which would be

contemplated by the ordinary consumer who purchases it, with the ordinary knowledge common to the community as to its characteristics.

Nevertheless, others took the inclusion of the phrase the phrase "unreasonably dangerous" as re-emphasizing that the plaintiff should have to prove negligence. Some supported this requirement; others, included the Supreme Court of California itself, remained implacably opposed. This issue became a particular bone of contention when the ALI decided that it was time to draft a Third Restatement.

5.5 The Third (or Products Liability) Restatement

By the 1990s, the ALI had concluded that much of the Second Restatement of Torts had become significantly out of date. But, rather than attempt to redraft the whole thing in one go, which would have been a mammoth task, it decided instead to break the law into parts and address them one by one. It had become clear, in particular, that products liability law could not be adequately encapsulated into just one section, and so it was decided that the field to be addressed first would be products liability.

At the same time, the ALI decided to adopt a new approach to drafting the text of the Restatement. As before, Reporters were appointed to write the text, but the group to whom they would report and from whom they would take direction was no longer confined to ALI members. Instead, that group was opened up to practitioners representing plaintiffs and product manufacturers. What followed was a series of meetings that were arguably the most contentious in the Institute's history, while the resulting document was certainly its most controversial publication.

Those who favor the Third Restatement of Torts: Products Liability (often referred to as the Products Liability Restatement) see it as a milestone along the road to what they call "tort reform." Its opponents see it as "tort *de*form." The Products Liability Restatement has become the most widely-quoted Restatement ever so far as the judiciary is concerned, but it is not always quoted with approval. Indeed, it has arguably been quoted almost as often because judges want to disparage it as inaccurate. The ALI appears to have reveled in this notoriety and has continued with the same approach of inviting practitioners to take part in ALI meetings at which the drafting of other Restatements is discussed.

The original purpose of the Restatements seems, however, to have become a casualty of the ALI's desire for the spotlight. That purpose had been to provide in one document a clear, comprehensive, and authoritative guide to the law in most states. Instead, products liability law has become bedeviled by a controversy over whether the Second or Third Restatement provides an accurate picture of the law.

The source of the controversy is this. Whereas section 402A of the Second Restatement was intended to give effect to Traynor's idea of strict products liability in torts, much of the Third Restatement would turn the clock back to before *Greenman* and reinstate the requirement for the plaintiff to prove negligence. Some states continue to favor the former; others have chosen to adopt the latter. Accordingly, in Chapters 6, 7, and 8, this book will address manufacturing defects, design defects, and failures to warn respectively from the perspective of both the Second and Third Restatements.

5.6 When "Strict Liability" Is Not Strict

Both Restatements agree that manufacturing defects involve strict liability, though the courts interpreting them do not necessarily agree on the practical ramifications. But in jurisdictions that have chosen to adopt the Third Restatement, talk of "strict" products liability in other contexts is apt to be highly misleading since, without proof of fault, the defendant cannot be found liable for either a design defect or a failure to warn.

Yet the label "strict products liability" remains in use in those jurisdictions. Readers should be aware that the word "strict" in this context does no work; the label actually signifies nothing more than "products liability," and the prefix "strict" is just redundant verbiage. In those jurisdictions, products liability is almost always predicated on a finding of fault, specifically negligence.

Nevertheless, the nomenclature used in the Third Restatement to denote different types of product defect has been adopted across the board. Every state now distinguishes between "manufacturing defects," "design defects," and "failures to warn." Chapters 6, 7, and 8 reflect these distinctions.

5.7 The Practical Implications of the Controversy

It is worth summarizing the practical implications of the differences between the approaches of the Second and Third Restatements because they are aired in almost every products liability case that proceeds to a full trial.

The most obvious implication is that plaintiffs generally prefer the Second Restatement because of its emphasis on strict liability, while defendants generally prefer the Third Restatement because of its insistence that the plaintiff needs to prove negligence. But it is essential to understand that, despite rhetoric to the contrary, this is not always true.

When the plaintiff is alleging a manufacturing defect, for example, they will typically be in a better position to make their case under the Third Restatement than under the Second. This is because of the need to establish "unreasonable danger" under the Second Restatement, whereas the Third Restatement imposes no such requirement.

A plaintiff may also be better off under the Third Restatement in a small number of cases of alleged design defects. This is because of the difference in focus of the two Restatements, which sees the Second concentrate on the state of the product, whereas the Third focuses on the nature of the defendant's conduct. While the Second Restatement's approach will be significantly more advantageous to the plaintiff in most instances, the approach of the Third Restatement will occasionally work to the plaintiff's advantage if its requirement to prove the unreasonableness of the defendant's conduct will be less onerous than the Second Restatement's requirement to prove the unreasonableness of the danger created.

5.7.1 Multiple Defendants

It is also important to know that a defendant's perspective as to which is the better Restatement to follow will often depend on whether it is the sole defendant or one among several. A singular defendant will naturally favor the very opposite of whichever approach favors the plaintiff. But when there is more than one defendant, the picture becomes rather more complex.

Plaintiffs do not prosecute a lawsuit in order just to win. They want to actually get paid—and so do their attorneys, who are typically working on a contingency fee basis. A plaintiff's strategy when bringing suit against multiple defendants is, therefore, designed less to maximize the headline figure of compensation awarded by a court and more to maximize the sum of money actually received. To this end, when a plaintiff sues several defendants in one action, they will typically be prepared to settle with the smaller defendants for the coverage limits of the defendant's insurance policy, and then seek to recover any other compensation—and, potentially, punitive damages—from the larger defendant, who is in a better financial position to actually pay up.

This means that—perhaps counter-intuitively—the interests of the smaller defendant in such circumstances will actually align with the interests of the plaintiff rather than with the interests of the larger defendant. This is because the easier it is for the plaintiff to establish the liability of the larger defendant, the less reason they will have to pursue the smaller defendant for anything more than the coverage limits of their insurance policy. In other words, smaller "Mom and Pop" business defendants will often be in a better position under the Second Restatement than under the Third.

SECOND VS THIRD RESTATEMENTS CHECKPOINTS

- Actions in contracts:
    - Do not require proof of fault, because liability is strict.
    - Require proof of some sort of horizontal and/or vertical privity.
    - Enable claims of compensation for harm done to the defective product itself.
    - Are not permitted to include claims for punitive damages.
- Actions in torts:
    - Require proof of fault.
    - Do not require that the parties to the litigation be in privity of contract.
    - May not include claims for compensation for harm done to the defective product itself because of the economic loss rule.
    - Enable claims to be made for punitive damages.

- The Second Restatement:
  - Focuses not on what the defendant did, but on whether the product was defective or not.
  - Treats all product defects as matters of strict liability.
  - Is generally more favorable to plaintiffs, except in cases of manufacturing defects.
- The Third (Products Liability) Restatement:
  - Treats manufacturing defects as a matter of strict liability with no need to prove that the product concerned is unreasonably dangerous.
  - Reintroduces the need to prove the defendant's negligence in cases of design defects and failures to warn, and so renders redundant the word "strict" in the phrase "strict products liability."
  - Is generally more favorable to defendants, except in cases of manufacturing defects or when there is more than one defendant (in which case, the smaller defendant will typically prefer the approach of the Second Restatement).

CHAPTER 6

Manufacturing Defects

MANUFACTURING DEFECTS ROADMAP

- Understand the difference between the foreign-natural and consumer expectations tests in food cases
- Understand the practical ramifications of bringing an action in contracts versus torts
- Understand the differences between the approaches of the Second and Third Restatements

---

6.1 Food

While the law of products liability has become extremely controversial and highly politicized since the publication of the Third (Products Liability) Restatement, it is undeniable that its recognition of three different types of product defects in section 1 has been universally accepted. This declares:

> A product is defective when, at the time of sale or distribution, it contains a manufacturing defect, is defective in design, or is defective because of inadequate instructions or warnings.

This chapter addresses manufacturing defects. As Justice Traynor recognized in *Greenman v. Yuba Power Products, Inc.*, 59 Cal. 2d 57, 62 (1963), the earliest successful cases all revolved around "unwholesome food products." This much is uncontroversial. But there has been a long-running debate over *how* to determine whether food is defective. The Supreme Court of Minnesota considered the issue in *Schafer v. J.L.C. Food Systems, Inc.*, 695 N.W.2d 570, 573–74 (Minn. 2005):

> We note that courts across the country have diverged on the proper test to apply in determining whether food containing an injurious object is actionable. Some courts follow what has been referred to as the foreign-natural test, while others have adopted what has become known as the reasonable expectation test....
>
> The foreign-natural test draws a distinction between the foreign and natural characteristics of a food product ingredient. Under the test, if an object or substance in a food product is natural to any of the ingredients of the product, there is no liability for injuries caused; if the object or substance is foreign to any of the ingredients, the seller or manufacturer of the product may be liable for any injury caused....
>
> Comparatively, the reasonable expectation test focuses on what is reasonably expected by the consumer in the food product as served, not what might be foreign or natural to the ingredients of that product before preparation.

6.1.1 Consumer Expectations Test

The *Schafer* court chose, 695 NW 2d 570, 575 (2005), to adopt the more widely-accepted reasonable expectation test, which harks back to Comment *i* to section 402A(1) of the Second Restatement. Consumer expectations:

> are based on culturally defined, widely shared standards allowing a seller's liability to be resolved by judges and triers of fact based on their assessment of what consumers have a right to expect from preparation of the food in question.

In fact, the Second Restatement adopted the consumer expectations test for determining whether *any* product is defective. As will shortly be seen, the Products Liability Restatement generally rejects that view. In cases involving food, however, section 7 of the Products Liability Restatement also takes the position that the appropriate test for determining defectiveness is the consumer expectations test.

6.1.2 Foreign-Natural Test

There are still some states, however, that use the foreign-natural test. In *Berkheimer v. REKM, LLC*, 2024 Ohio 2787 (2024), for example, the Supreme Court of Ohio reaffirmed the application of the foreign-natural test. It went on to hold that a consumer who got a 2-inch long chicken bone lodged in his esophagus after eating what purported to be "boneless" wings did not have a cause of action against the restaurant who served them, since chicken bones are not foreign to chicken. Despite widespread ridicule of its decision that "boneless" wings means "wings that may contain bones," the court confirmed its decision on rehearing by the same 4–3 majority.

Even more significantly, the court considered this to be a matter of law. It therefore affirmed summary judgment for the restaurant, so that the plaintiff was not permitted to put his case to a jury.

6.1.3 Emotional Distress

Chapter 1 spelled out the five elements that a plaintiff must establish in order to be successful in a products liability lawsuit. One of those was the need to prove actual or imminent physical harm (whether personal injury or damage to property). There has never been any doubt that someone who can show that they have suffered personal injury can also include any resultant emotional distress in their claim. This is hardly surprising; someone who loses a limb, for example, may suffer significant emotional distress in additional to the personal injury.

Claims for emotional distress that are *not* predicated on personal injury have, however, typically been rejected by the courts. Three reasons have typically been articulated for this:

- The prospect of indeterminate liability
- The lack of an objective standard for quantifying claims
- The possibility of fraudulent claims

The issue with indeterminate liability is that, when one person suffers an injury, it may have a significant emotional effect on all those around them. Allowing such claims would then multiply the number of plaintiffs significantly and correspondingly increase the amount of compensation to be paid out.

Secondly, it is hard to identify objectively when someone suffers emotional distress. It cannot, for example, be proved by photographs or X-rays. And even if the existence of such distress is not in doubt, it is still not clear how it can be objectively measured. Yet, without such a measure, there is no way to know how much money should be paid as compensation.

Such lack of objectivity leads to a third problem, namely the possibility of fraudulent claims. If there is no objective standard by which to measure a claim of emotional distress, it is hard to be sure that such a claim is not entirely bogus.

6.1.4 New Approach?

It is worth noting, however, that those problems with claims for emotional distress do not carry the same weight when the person making such claims is the primary victim of the defective product rather than a secondary victim whose distress is caused by the *primary* victim's injury. If the person making the claim is the primary victim, then there is no prospect of indeterminate liability, and the likelihood of fraud is significantly reduced.

That leaves only the problem of quantifying claims. But quantifying claims for personal injuries often suffers from precisely the same problem, and yet the law does not shy away from awarding compensation for, for example, paralysis or loss of a limb. Moreover, as previously acknowledged, the law is content to allow claims for emotional distress that arise from personal injury, yet the existence of prior physical harm hardly makes the amount of distress sustained easier to quantify.

In *Bylsma v. Burger King Corp.*, the plaintiff sought to claim compensation for emotional distress after a burger he ordered was contaminated with the spit of one of the restaurant's employees. He had suspected that the burger was contaminated before eating it, and so had not consumed any of it. He had, therefore, suffered no physical harm. The Supreme Court of Washington, *en banc*, nevertheless held, 293 P.3d 1168, 1171 (Wash. 2013):

> Common sense tells us that food consumption is a personal matter and contaminated food is closely associated with disgust and other kinds of emotional turmoil. Thus, when a food manufacturer serves a contaminated food product, it is well within the scope of foreseeable harmful consequences that the individual served will suffer emotional distress. The courts of this state recognize damages for such emotional distress, and thus, such damages, if proved, are recoverable.

It is noteworthy that, once again, food was treated differently from other products.

6.2 Strict Liability Reaffirmed

As for those other products, chapter 5 explored how the Supreme Court of California, led by Justice Roger Traynor, led a movement to make products liability strict rather than dependent on a finding of the defendant's negligence. It also explained how section 402A(1) of the Second Restatement of Torts then sought to summarize the effect of cases like *Greenman* and *Vandermark v. Ford Motor Co.*, 61 Cal. 2d 256 (1964), by stating that a product liability claim involves a product being "in a defective condition unreasonably dangerous to the user or consumer or to his property."

In *Cronin v. J.B.E. Olson Corp.*, the Supreme Court of California was strongly critical of the inclusion of the words "unreasonably dangerous" in section 402A. Writing for the court, Justice Sullivan observed, 8 Cal. 3d 121, 132–33 (1972):

> [I]t has burdened the injured plaintiff with proof of an element which rings of negligence....
>
> Of particular concern is the susceptibility of Restatement section 402A to a literal reading which would require the finder of fact to conclude that the product is, first, defective and, second, unreasonably dangerous. A bifurcated standard is of necessity more difficult to prove than a unitary one. But merely proclaiming that the phrase defective condition unreasonably dangerous requires only a single finding would not purge that phrase of its negligence complexion. We think that a requirement that a plaintiff also prove that the defect made the product unreasonably dangerous places upon him a significantly increased burden and represents a step backward in the area pioneered by this court.

Accordingly, the court reaffirmed its view that the plaintiff simply has to show that their injury was caused by a product that was defective, and that was to be determined according to the expectations of the reasonable consumer. There was no additional requirement to prove that the defect involved the prospect of unreasonable danger.

But Justice Sullivan went further. In a passage displaying remarkable foresight of developments that were to occur over twenty years later, he added, 8 Cal. 3d 121, 134 (1972):

> We can see no difficulty in applying the *Greenman* formulation to the full range of products liability situations, including those involving "de-

sign defects." A defect may emerge from the mind of the designer as well as from the hand of the workman....

The most obvious problem we perceive in creating any such distinction is that thereafter it would be advantageous to characterize a defect in one rather than the other category. It is difficult to prove that a product ultimately caused injury because a widget was poorly welded—a defect in manufacture—rather than because it was made of inexpensive metal difficult to weld, chosen by a designer concerned with economy—a defect in design.... We wish to avoid providing such a battleground for clever counsel. Furthermore, we find no reason why a different standard, and one harder to meet, should apply to defects which plague entire product lines.

6.3 The Third (Products Liability) Restatement

Justice Sullivan's concerns are precisely those voiced in opposition to the text of much of the Third Restatement of Torts: Products Liability. Published in 1998, this divided product defects into manufacturing defects, design defects, and failures to warn. As Sullivan had predicted, the reason for doing so was precisely to apply a different test for what constitutes a defect to each type. The notion of applying the consumer expectations test across the board was abandoned. Instead, the need to prove negligence was largely reinstated.

The one significant exception to that last statement concerns manufacturing defects. Section 2(a) of the Third Restatement declares that they occur "when the product departs from its intended design." But while this certainly does not re-impose a negligence requirement, it still—except in cases involving food or used products—represents a clear rejection of the consumer expectations test.

Instead, section 2(a) creates a sort of "manufacturer's expectations" test. That is because it is first necessary to discern what the manufacturer intended before it is possible to work out whether the specific product matches that intent.

6.3.1 Changing Back the Focus

The significance of this approach is that, even when not talking in terms of negligence, the Products Liability Restatement seeks to restore the focus to the defendant, where it had been before *Greenman*.

When talking of design defects and failures to warn, it focuses on the defendant's conduct, just as would be the case in a regular negligence lawsuit. For manufacturing defects, while conceding that this should be an area of strict liability, it still manages to focus on the defendant by insisting that the first thing to establish is the defendant's original intent when designing the product.

This defendant focus means that the defendant is fully in control of whether they will be liable for harm caused by one of their products. That is very different from the consumer expectations test, where the arbiter of what is defective is the general public, as represented by the jury. Proponents of the Third Restatement argue that it is fairer because it helps to avoid the floodgates problems noted in Chapter 1; the defendant is effectively in charge of deciding what risks to run.

Critics argue that it is not fairer for many of the victims of defective products, who never have any realistic prospect of deciding what risks to run. Moreover, the consumer expectations test is more appropriate, they argue, because it mirrors the approach taken by the law of contracts for breach of warranty. And the Products Liability Restatement completely ignores Justice Traynor's point in *Escola v. Coca Cola Bottling Co.*, 24 Cal. 2d 453, 456 (1944), that, in a case where both the plaintiff and defendant are innocent of any blame, it makes the most sense to have the cost of such harm borne by the defendant, because they are in the best position to bear it.

6.3.2 Products Liability Restatement in Action

Justice Sullivan in *Cronin* had also presciently pointed out that recognizing different categories of defect would open the way to manufacturers avoiding responsibility by claiming in a specific case that the defect in question should be considered of one type and not another. To put it simply, the Third Restatement enables manufacturers to claim: "It's not a bug, it's a feature."

If they can successfully argue that the product defect in question was actually part of the design, then the plaintiff will need to prove that the design was negligent. Whereas, if the defect is categorized as one of manufacture, any departure from the intended design is proof of a defect, regardless of how reasonably or otherwise the defendant behaved.

The case of *Oglesby v. Medtronic, Inc.*, Case No. 23-50274 (5th Cir. Mar. 26, 2024), provides an unfortunate example. In July 2019, Oglesby had surgery to address a cyst on her cervical spine. During the surgery, Oglesby's physician implanted a Durepair Dura Regeneration Matrix—a medical device designed to be used as a patch to repair dura matter, which is a membrane protecting the brain and spinal cord. Soon after the surgery, Oglesby experienced severe headaches and other serious symptoms. Oglesby underwent another surgery in which her physician discovered that the Durepair patch had largely disintegrated, causing a cerebrospinal fluid leak.

Before the publication of the Products Liability Restatement, the plaintiff's claim of manufacturing defect would have succeeded. The Durepair patch had clearly not met consumer expectations.

But with focus shifted back to the defendant under the Products Liability Restatement, the Fifth Circuit was content to affirm summary judgment in favor of the defendants on the grounds that Oglesby had not attempted to identify any specific way in which the Durepair product deviated from its design. As if it had been designed to disintegrate!

6.4 Used Products

Defects in used products are—like food—to be judged according to the consumer expectations test, even under the Products Liability Restatement.

Section 8 of that Restatement defines a used product as one that has been "commercially sold or otherwise distributed to a buyer not in the commercial chain of distribution and used for some period of time" before the transaction involved in the case at hand. Subsection (b) makes clear that someone engaged in the business of selling or otherwise distributing used products may be liable if they sell a used product that contains a manufacturing defect. (The Second Restatement made no distinction between sellers of new and used products.)

This might seem somewhat draconian. But, to avoid treating used products as if they were new, an additional element must be proved. The seller's marketing of the product must have been such as to cause cause a reasonable buyer "to expect the used product to present no greater risk of defect than if the product were new." Auto dealerships selling "pre-owned" vehicles that have gone through multi-point checks before being advertised for sale are classic examples.

This effectively reintroduces the consumer expectations test. While it might be argued that those expectations are now to be addressed only for a comparison between the used product and its likely defects (or absence thereof), this inevitably means that the consumer needs to have some expectations of the product when new. Which is precisely the test that, except for food, was otherwise abandoned in section 2(a)!

Some courts have imposed strict liability on commercial sellers of used products because they have found that the public policy that encourages product safety applies just as much to them as to brand new products. A used product may not last as long, or work as efficiently, but there is no reason for it to be unsafe. Sellers should not be able, for example, to sell used cars with defective brakes without the risk of incurring liability if those brakes cause a crash.

Other courts have been prepared to impose liability for defective used products only if the seller knew of the defect or had a legal obligation to inspect the product before sale. In some states, whether the original manufacturer is solvent and susceptible to jurisdiction is also a relevant factor.

6.5 Economic Loss Rule Revisited

The Supreme Court of California in *Cronin* remained steadfast in its view that liability for a defective product in torts is strict, just like claims for breach of warranty in contracts. This inevitably raised the question of whether the court would be prepared to adopt any other features hitherto characteristic only of contract law. In *Seely v. White Motor Co.*, the plaintiff had bought a truck that turned out to be a "lemon." He sued on the basis of breach of warranty and was awarded compensation for his losses including loss of profits. By this time, Traynor had become the Chief Justice of the Supreme Court of California. Writing for the Court, he held, 63 Cal. 2d 9, 15 (1965):

> It is contended that the foregoing legislative scheme of recovery has been superseded by the doctrine of strict liability in tort set forth in *Greenman v. Yuba Power Products, Inc.* and *Vandermark v. Ford Motor Co.* We

> cannot agree with this contention. The law of sales has been carefully articulated to govern the economic relations between suppliers and consumers of goods. The history of the doctrine of strict liability in tort indicates that it was designed, not to undermine the warranty provisions of the sales act or of the Uniform Commercial Code but, rather, to govern the distinct problem of physical injuries....
>
> The distinction that the law has drawn between tort recovery for physical injuries and warranty recovery for economic loss is not arbitrary.... A consumer should not be charged at the will of the manufacturer with bearing the risk of physical injury when he buys a product on the market. He can, however, be fairly charged with the risk that the product will not match his economic expectations unless the manufacturer agrees that it will. Even in actions for negligence, a manufacturer's liability is limited to damages for physical injuries and there is no recovery for economic loss alone.

In other words, the court held that the economic loss rule continues to apply to torts cases where the harm is suffered by the defective product itself. Compensation for such losses remains recoverable only in the law of contracts.

This position was confirmed more recently by the Supreme Court of Tennessee, which observed in *Lincoln General Ins. v. Detroit Diesel Corp.*, 293 S.W.3d 487, 491 (2009):

> We agree ... that the owner of a defective product that creates a risk of injury and was damaged during a fire, a crash, or other similar occurrence is in the same position as the owner of a defective product that malfunctions and simply does not work. It follows that the remedies available to these similarly situated product owners should derive from the parties' agreements, not from the law of torts, lest we disrupt the parties' allocation of risk.

Only *actual* harm to persons or property *other than* the defective product itself avoids the clutches of the economic loss rule. The fact that the product is now in a state that makes it likely to cause such harm in the future makes no difference. Compensation to pay for remedial work to render the product safe must, therefore, be sought through a claim for breach of warranty in contracts.

6.6 Components

This raises the question of how the law should deal with a complex product which is made of many different components, and which suffers damage only because one of those components is defective. Should the law treat the complex product as one entity, or as a collection of separate products?

Section 5 of the Products Liability Restatement makes it clear that, if a component is integrated into a larger product and a defect in the component then causes the larger product to harm a reasonably foreseeable user or consumer (or their property), the component manufacturer will be liable for that harm. This does not, however, provide a defense for the manufacturer of the larger product, since they will also be liable if they played a more than minimal role in integrating the component into the design of the larger product.

But what if the defective component causes harm to some other part of the larger product into which it has been integrated? *Jimenez v. Superior Court*, 127 Cal. Rptr. 2d 614 (Cal. 2002), was such a case. A window manufacturer had installed its windows throughout a new housing development. But the windows leaked and caused damage to other parts of the homes, including stucco, insulation, framing, drywall, and baseboards. The plaintiffs sought to claim compensation for manufacturing defects with the windows, but the defendants argued that a house is an entire, integrated product, of which the windows were an integral part, so that the defective windows had caused only damage to the defective product itself.

In an influential concurrence in the Supreme Court of California, Justice Kennard considered two cases decided by the United States Supreme Court. The first was *East River S.S. Corp. v. Transamerica Delaval*, 476 U.S. 858 (1986). Justice Kennard, 127 Cal. Rptr. 2d 614, 625 (2002), described it as a case where:

> [C]ompanies that chartered oil-transporting supertankers brought an action under maritime law seeking to hold a turbine manufacturer strictly liable in tort for income losses and repair costs resulting when a defective part of the supertankers' turbines damaged other parts of the turbines.... The Court determined that the defective part of the turbine had been so integrated into the turbine that it lost its separate identity, and thus the manufacturer was not strictly liable in tort for injury that the component part caused to the turbine....

The second case was *Saratoga Fishing Co. v. J.M. Martinac & Co.*, 520 U.S. 875 (1997), where a skiff, a net, and various spare parts had been added to a ship after its original sale. The question was whether this equipment was property *other than* the ship itself so as to permit recovery for the loss of these items when the ship caught fire and sank. The Court held that it was; the extra equipment had not been so integrated into the ship that it had lost its separate identity.

The Supreme Court of California found *Saratoga* to be more apposite. Justice Kennard pointed out, 127 Cal. Rptr. 2d 614, 626 (2002), that: "Windows can be readily removed from houses and replaced with other windows. A window that has been removed from one house can then be installed in another house." Accordingly, the economic loss rule was held to be inapplicable.

MANUFACTURING DEFECTS CHECKPOINTS

- Liability for a manufacturing defect is strict under both the Second and Third Restatements of Torts.
- Under the Second Restatement, a manufacturing defect occurs when the product fails to meet reasonable consumer expectations.
- Under the Third Restatement, a manufacturing defect occurs when the product differs from its intended design.
- Liability under the Second Restatement of Torts requires proof that the product defect was "unreasonably dangerous," although many states that purport to have adopted the Second Restatement do not recognize that requirement as part of their law.
- Liability under the Third Restatement does not require proof that the product defect was "unreasonably dangerous."
- The test for whether food is defective is determined by the "consumer expectations" test under either Restatement.
- A primary (but not secondary) victim of contaminated food, but not of other defective products, may also be able to claim for emotional distress, even if the product itself caused them no physical harm.
- Under both the Second and Third Restatements of Torts, the economic loss rule in torts continues to bar claims for compensation for harm caused to the defective product itself.

- Liability for the manufacture or distribution of a defective component depends on the degree to which it was integrated into a larger product.
- Liability for a manufacturing defect in a used product depends on the reasonable consumer expectations generated by the seller's marketing of the product. It may also depend on whether:
  - The seller knew of the defect or had a legal obligation to inspect the product.
  - The original manufacturer is solvent and susceptible to jurisdiction.

CHAPTER 7

Design Defects

DESIGN DEFECTS ROADMAP

- Understand the difference between the consumer expectations and risk-utility tests, and how they may sometimes be combined
- Understand the practical ramifications of the reasonable alternative design requirement
- Understand how design defects may involve strict liability or proof of negligence, according to the jurisdiction

---

7.1 Consumer Expectations Test

Section 402A of the Second Restatement of Torts draws no distinctions between different types of product defect. Accordingly, what we now think of as design defects are to be judged by exactly the same test as that used to determine manufacturing defects: the consumer expectations test. Adopting the same approach means that manufacturers cannot defend a claim that one of their products is defective by arguing that it was supposed to behave like that. It is not within their power to determine how the product should behave; that is a question for the reasonable consumer. Under the Second Restatement of Torts, therefore, it is for the reasonable consumer (as represented by a jury) to determine whether a product's design is sound or defective.

In *Green v. Smith & Nephew A.H.P., Inc.*, 629 N.W.2d 727 (Wisc. 2001), for example, Green, a health worker, developed a severe rash, peeling skin, acute shortness of breath, coughing, and tightening of the throat so severe as to cause her to spend significant time in hospital. It turned out she had developed an allergy to latex from the latex gloves she had been wearing. Green sued the manufacturer, arguing:

1. the gloves contained excessive levels of allergy-causing latex proteins; and
2. the cornstarch with which Smith & Nephew powdered its gloves increased the likelihood that persons would inhale the latex proteins, making it much more likely to cause an allergic reaction.

Smith & Nephew argued that the proper test for defectiveness of the gloves should include factors beyond consumer expectations. The Supreme Court of Wisconsin disagreed. It emphasized that the consumer expectations test is not dependent upon the knowledge of the particular injured consumer but is instead to be assessed from the point of view of a *reasonable* consumer. Since the jury represents the reasonable consumer, and it had found that the latex gloves did not meet consumer expectations, the court affirmed judgment in favor of Green.

7.2 Risk-Utility Test

At the time that Green began experiencing her injuries, the health care community generally was unaware that persons could develop an allergy to latex. So *Green* may fairly be cited as an example of a case where neither party was at fault. In such cases, as Judge Traynor noted decades ago, it is really a policy question of whether it should be the victim or the defendant who bears the loss. Yet, as Professor David G. Owen has noted, *Products Liability*, in *The Philosophy of Law: An Encyclopedia* Vol. 2 (C.B. Gray ed., 1999) at 690, it remains the case that:

> One of the most perplexing doctrinal problems in products liability law today is the question of who should bear responsibility for risks that neither party fairly could expect.

It should, therefore, come as no surprise that product manufacturers, sellers, and their insurers mounted a powerful campaign to modify the law's approach to design defects. They argued instead for what they called a "risk-utility" test. This has often been said to involve an evaluation of the following factors:

- The product's utility to the user and to the public as a whole;
- The likelihood that the product will cause injury, and the likely severity of the injury;

- The availability of a safer alternative design;
- The ability to remove the alleged unsafe character of the product without impeding the product's usefulness or making it too expensive to maintain its utility;
- The user's ability to avoid danger by exercising care in use of the product;
- The user's anticipated awareness of the product's danger because of the obvious condition of the product or as a result of warnings or instructions; and
- The ability of the manufacturer to spread the loss by setting the price of the product or carrying liability insurance.

7.2.1 No Alternative?

The Reporters for the Products Liability Restatement agreed. They took the view that the continuity of approach between manufacturing and design defects was not sustainable. In Comment *a* to section 1 of the Products Liability Restatement, they argued that:

> [I]t soon became apparent that § 402A [of the Second Restatement] ... could not appropriately be applied to cases of design defects.... A product unit that fails to meet the manufacturer's design specifications thereby fails to perform its intended function and is, almost by definition, defective. However, when the product unit meets the manufacturer's own design specifications, it is necessary to go outside those specifications to determine whether the product is defective.

Note, however, that the apparent justification given in the last sentence for applying a different approach to different types of product defect depends on the assertion in the second sentence being true. If, instead, the second sentence's reference to "the manufacturer's design specifications" is replaced by the phrase, "reasonable consumer expectations," the purported justification falls flat.

In other words, the justification offered in Comment *a* works only if it is accepted that the focus of products liability cases should be on the defendant. If, by contrast, the focus should be on the plaintiff or on the public more generally, then it provides no justification at all. As already noted, preference for one test over the other is not a matter of inexorable logic. It is simply a policy choice.

The policy favored by the Reporters for the Products Liability Restatement is embodied in section 2(b). It declares that a product:

> is defective in design when the foreseeable risks of harm posed by the product could have been reduced or avoided by the adoption of a reasonable alternative design by the seller or other distributor, or a predecessor in the commercial chain of distribution, and the omission of the alternative design renders the product not reasonably safe....

As should, by now, be clear, this focuses the defect inquiry squarely on the defendant. In doing so, it also re-imposes on the plaintiff a requirement to prove negligence. Indeed, it arguably goes even further than that by requiring proof not just of one, but of *two* types of unreasonableness: the failure to "adopt[] a reasonable alternative design" and the product being "not reasonably safe." Justice Roger Traynor would have been horrified! As noted in Chapter 5, the nature of the defendant's conduct was, for him, immaterial.

Moreover, if it were true that the Second Restatement consumer expectations test "could not appropriately be applied to cases of design defects or defects based on inadequate instructions or warnings," every state in the nation would have had no choice but to embrace the Products Liability Restatement. Yet that has simply not happened. Most recently, the Supreme Court of Appeals of West Virginia announced in *Shears v. Ethicon, Inc.*, 902 S.E.2d 775 (W. Va. 2024), that "we reject the definition of a design defect set out in the [Products Liability] Restatement § 2."

7.2.2 Efficiency

Since the justification for section 2(b) provided by Comment *a* is so weak, it is probably not surprising that other justifications have been offered too. One is that section 2(b) promotes efficiency much better than section 402A of the Second Restatement of Torts. Professor David G. Owen once put it this way:

> When a consumer's prior expectations concerning product safety are fractured by an accident, and the manufacturer did not affirmatively create the unmet expectations, principles of utility and efficiency should help define a moral basis for deciding liability.... The principle of utility dictates that actors seek to maximize communal welfare and, commen-

> surately, that they seek to minimize waste. If a consumer suffers injury from an inefficient product risk—one that was excessive for the benefits achieved—the manufacturer may be faulted on moral grounds for causing waste (assuming that it was feasible to reduce the risk). However, if the maker carefully and fairly determines that the benefits of a particular design exceed its inherent dangers, then consumers who suffer injury unavoidably from those dangers may not fairly challenge the manufacturer's "legislative" design decision, a decision which was proper by hypothesis.

Products Liability, in *The Philosophy of Law: An Encyclopedia* Vol. 2 (C.B. Gray ed., 1999) at 690–91.

As a matter of principle, this argument sounds promising. As a matter of practice, however, it is hopeless. Judge Learned Hand pointed out decades ago, *Moisan v. Loftus*, 178 F.2d 148, 149 (2d Cir. 1949), that a court is in no position to be able to make a "quantitative estimate" of all the variables that this sort of calculation of efficiency entails, so that "[i]t follows that all such attempts are illusory."

Indeed, in the notorious Ford Pinto lawsuit, *Grimshaw v. Ford Motor Co.*, 119 Cal. App. 3d 757 (1981), Ford purported to compare the total safety benefit of relocating the badly-placed gas tank with the cost of relocating it. This was, however, ruled inadmissible in evidence because it involved Ford simply asserting monetary sums like the dollar value of a human life.

The efficiency argument might sound good in an academic ivory tower, but it carries little weight in the legal system.

7.2.3 Beyond Consumers' Competence

In fact, the strongest argument in favor of the adoption of section 2(b) as the test of design defect is that many designs involve issues that are far beyond the competence of consumers to judge. As Justice Baxter of the Supreme Court of California noted, *Soule v. General Motors Corp.*, 8 Cal. 4th 548, 566–67 (1994), thirty years ago:

> [A] complex product, even when it is being used as intended, may often cause injury in a way that does not engage its ordinary consumers' reasonable minimum assumptions about safe performance. For example, the ordinary consumer of an automobile simply has "no idea" how it

> should perform in all foreseeable situations, or how safe it should be made against all foreseeable hazards.

For this reason many states apply the consumer expectations test when assessing an alleged product defect that is within the competence of a reasonable consumer, but use the risk-utility test in other cases.

But other states have taken a different tack. In *Green* for example, the Supreme Court of Wisconsin made a similar observation, 629 N.W.2d 727, 804–05 (Wis. 2001), to that of Justice Baxter in *Soule*. Yet that did not make it adopt the risk-utility test for cases where assessing the alleged product defect is beyond the competence of a reasonable consumer. Instead "the inquiry in those cases must focus on whether the design features present an unreasonable danger to the ordinary consumer." This demonstrates an interesting application of section 402A of the Second Restatement, for it transforms the "unreasonable danger" requirement into its own test to be used only in cases beyond the day-to-day competence of the reasonable consumer.

Connecticut has taken yet another approach, which combines the consumer expectations and risk-utility tests, plus the "unreasonable danger" requirement, into a two-step process that it calls a "modified" consumer expectation test. This requires that the jury:

> weigh the product's risks and utility and then inquire, in light of those factors, whether a reasonable consumer would consider the product design unreasonably dangerous.

Izzarelli v. R.J. Reynolds Tobacco Co., 136 A.3d 1232, 1242 (Conn. 2016).

Yet, whichever test—or combination of tests—is applied, the economic loss rule remains in effect.

7.3 Reasonable Alternative Design

From the point of view of both its judicial and academic critics, the main problem with section 2(b) of the Products Liability Restatement is its claim that a design defect requires that the plaintiff prove that the foreseeable risks of harm by the product could have been reduced or avoided by the adoption of a reasonable alternative design. In *Vautour v. Body Masters Sports Industries, Inc.*, the Supreme Court of New Hampshire voiced the approach taken by many states when it observed, 147 N.H. 150, 156 (2001): "while proof of an alternative design is relevant in a design defect case, it should be neither a controlling factor nor an essential element that must be proved in every case."

More recently, the Supreme Court of Nevada was even more blunt. In *Ford Motor Co. v. Trejo*, 402 P.3d 649, 651 (Nev. 2017), it declared:

> [T]his court strongly disagrees with the notion that a plaintiff in a strict product liability design defect action must present proof of an alternative design. Such a requirement unfairly raises a plaintiffs burden of proof, and in some cases, poses an insurmountable barrier to bringing a claim. Therefore, this court declines to adopt the risk-utility test for strict product liability design defect claims. Claims of design defect grounded on strict product liability in Nevada will continue to be governed by the consumer-expectation test.

7.3.1 Reasonableness

Two things make the reasonable alternative design requirement so controversial. One is its use of the word "reasonable." As the Supreme Court of Iowa emphasized in *Wright v. Brooke Group Ltd.*, 652 N.W.2d 159 (Ia. 2002), this means that the reasonable alternative design requirement involves rejection of strict liability for design defect cases and instead marks a return to liability based on negligence.

The Restatement does recognize one exception, however. Comment *e* to section 2 provides that the reasonable alternative design requirement does not apply when the product design is "manifestly unreasonable." This seems to be a way of permitting a form of *res ipsa loquitur* argument, although what is "manifest" might, like beauty, be in the eye of the beholder.

The reasonable alternative design test involves a two-step test. First, it requires that the plaintiff prove that an alternative design was available for the product in question. The most common way of doing this is by identifying a competitor who uses that design. Another method is to show that the defendant itself uses that design in a different product. In either case, expert witnesses will be needed both to justify the comparison and to explain how the alternative design could have been incorporated into the product at stake. The more complex the product, the greater the need for expert witnesses.

Secondly, the plaintiff must establish that it was reasonable for the manufacturer to adopt the alternative design. To put this another way, the reasonable alternative design test requires that the risks and utility of the alternative design be compared with the product's current design. "Reasonableness" in this context involves an evaluation of what the Eighth Circuit, *Hoppe v. Midwest Conveyor Company, Inc.*, 485 F.2d 1196, 1202 (8th Cir. 1973), once referred to as "the relative cost and feasibility" of adopting the alternative design. The cost of implementing the alternative design is, therefore, one of the factors to be taken into account. Yet there is no hard-and-fast rule on how much it would be reasonable to spend on implementing the alternative design. In the end, this is a matter for the judgment of the jury, informed by expert witnesses' estimation of the costs and benefits involved. Such an assessment can never be a perfect science.

7.3.2 Proving a Negative

The second controversial issue is that, even if the plaintiff can establish that there was a reasonable alternative product design available, section 2(b) dictates that the case will still fail unless it can be established that adopting that design would have prevented—or, at least, significantly reduced—the harm sustained.

The problem here is that this involves proving a negative: that something would *not* have happened. This may form an insurmountable stumbling block for those injured by badly designed products. It is certainly an extremely high hurdle to jump because a negative can never be proved directly. It must always be established through inference. For this reason, the Supreme Court of New Hampshire held in *Vautour*, 147 N.H. 150, 156 (2001) that "the rigid prerequisite of a reasonable alternative design places too much emphasis on one of many possible factors that could potentially affect the risk-utility analysis."

7.4 Compliance with Administrative Standards

Many products, from food to child car seats, are subject to some sort of regulation. As section 4(b) of the Products Liability Restatement points out, however, compliance with such standards "does not preclude as a matter of law a finding of product defect."

Section 4(b) also states, nevertheless, that such compliance "is properly considered in determining whether the product is defective." But not all states agree. In *Sullivan v. Werner Co.*, for example, the Supreme Court of Pennsylvania ruled that compliance evidence was inadmissible. Applying the risk-utility test, it argued, 306 A.3d 846, 861–62 (Pa. 2023):

> Compliance evidence does not prove any characteristic of the product; rather, it diverts attention from the product's attributes to both the manufacturer's conduct and whether a standards-issuing organization would consider the product to be free from defects. Neither of these considerations are pertinent to a risk-utility analysis.

7.5 Prescription Drugs and Medical Devices

One area where administrative regulation undoubtedly *is* relevant (even in Pennsylvania) is that concerning prescription drugs and medical devices. The reason is simple. These products can legitimately come to market *only* if they comply with the rules and directives of the Food and Drug Administration (FDA).

This fact also produces another consequence. While it has already been noted that the "reasonable alternative design" test is controversial, everyone agrees that it cannot be applied to prescription drugs. It is also rarely applicable to medical devices. This is because the test requires that there is a viable alternative design that would have been feasible to implement, yet that will not be true of any such drugs and most such devices.

These items become available to the general public only after they have been subjected to extensive clinical trials, which have themselves been reviewed by the FDA. Permitting a finding that an alternative formulation or specification should have been adopted would imply that a judge or jury could predict the outcome of clinical trials on a drug or device which might not yet even exist.

Moreover, even after clinical trials have been conducted, a drug or device cannot be made generally available unless it has first been formally approved and licensed by the FDA. A judge or jury cannot find that an alternative formulation or specification should have been used if that alternative design or formulation has not been licensed by the FDA.

The one potential exception relates to a medical device that is "substantially equivalent" to a device that has already been approved by the FDA. Such a device will itself be approved through an accelerated process, and so it may sometimes be possible for a plaintiff to argue for a reasonable alternative design that would be substantially equivalent to an existing device.

Agreement on the impossibility of using the reasonable alternative design test for any prescription drugs and most medical devices should not, however, be taken as suggesting that there is agreement on the test that should be used in its stead. Proponents of the Second Restatement of Torts, of course, advocate for the use of the consumer expectations test. The Reporters for the Products Liability Restatement, by contrast, drafted the following test in section 6(c):

> A prescription drug or medical device is not reasonably safe due to defective design if the foreseeable risks of harm posed by the drug or medical device are sufficiently great in relation to its foreseeable therapeutic benefits that reasonable health-care providers, knowing of such foreseeable risks and therapeutic benefits, would not prescribe the drug or medical device for any class of patients.

This imposes an exceptionally high burden of proof because it means that, so long as one "class of patients" benefits from the drug or device, then it can never be considered to have a design defect at all. Indeed, if Thalidomide had been made available in the US, this provision would have meant that its manufacturer could never have been sued for birth defects caused to children whose mothers were prescribed the drug for morning sickness because the drug is effective for treating leprosy.

Moreover, the size of a "class" has never been formally defined; it is unclear whether there could be a class of one.

7.6 State of the Art

Whichever test—or combination of tests—are used to determine whether a particular product suffers from a defective design, a defendant may sometimes argue that the design amounted to the best possible at the time. In other words, it represented the "state of the art."

Such a plea is arguably inapplicable to cases where the consumer expectations test is applied, since that test is concerned solely with whether such expectations were met. It is not interested in hearing any explanation as to why they were not.

But the notion of "state of the art" is effectively a trump card when the risk-utility test is implicated. If the design truly reflected the state of the art at the time when the product was made, then by definition no reasonable alternative design was available, and so the plaintiff's claim must be denied. The normal weighing of various factors to assess the competing risks and utility of the design is thus abandoned in favor of judgment as a matter of law for the defendant.

The plea that a design met the state of the art is not an affirmative defense. Such a defense enables a defendant to argue that, *despite* the plaintiff's having been able to prove every element of her claim, they should nevertheless not win the case.

A plea of "state of the art" is much more powerful. It argues that an essential element in the plaintiff's case has never been proved. For it argues that the design was simply not defective at all. If the plaintiff cannot prove that the product was defective, then clearly there is nothing on which a claim for product liability can be based.

Smith v. 2328 University Ave. Corp., 52 A.D.3d 216 (N.Y. App. Div. 2008), is a case in point. It involved an action for damages for injuries sustained by the infant plaintiffs as the result of their exposure to lead-based paint in the apartment where they resided between 1995 and 2001. While the litigation was pending, NL Industries was identified as the manufacturer of the paint pigments containing the lead used to make the paint that allegedly poisoned the infants, and so a second amended complaint alleged causes of action against NL for negligence and strict products liability. An appellate court in New York denied the claim, however, because any interior lead paint present in the plaintiffs' home was applied before 1960. This was the year when the manufacture, sale, and distribution of lead-based pigments and paint, and their use in residential units, was outlawed. Since the paint pigments manufactured by NL were not defective at the time they were created, nor was distribution thereof prohibited until 1960, there was no question of finding the manufacturer liable. Indeed, any injury that had arisen would have been due to poor maintenance of the property in failing to prevent the paint from peeling and flaking, at which point it would have become hazardous through possible ingestion or inhalation.

It is important to note, however, that a plea that a design represented the state of the art is very different from a claim that it reflected industry custom. A custom can still be evaluated to see whether a reasonable alternative design was available, whereas an effective plea that the design in question reflected the state of the art simply denies the validity of any such evaluation. This means, of course, that any such plea is typically hotly contested, with expert testimony inevitably involved.

7.7 Subsequent Remedial Measures

Hindsight is a wonderful thing. A seller or manufacturer of a product may believe that its design is safe and appropriate for the task for which it is intended, but then an accident occurs whose likelihood could clearly have been reduced or eliminated if some aspect of the design had been different.

The public interest is clearly best served by the seller or manufacturer modifying the design so as to make the product (and maybe others like it) safer, and so render another such accident less likely. But what if the original victim used such a modification to argue that it proves the original design was defective? The federal courts have concluded that that would obviously create an incentive for the seller and manufacturer to do nothing and so leave the product in a state that is more dangerous than it should be. As the Supreme Court of Minnesota observed over a century ago in *Morse v. Minneapolis & St. Louis Ry. Co.*, 30 Minn. 465, 469 (1883), it would "virtually hold[] out an inducement for continued negligence."

In order to avoid that problem, the courts developed a rule that made evidence of subsequent remedial measures inadmissible as a means of proving a product defect. It is now codified in the federal system in Federal Rule of Evidence 407:

> When measures are taken that would have made an earlier injury or harm less likely to occur, evidence of the subsequent measures is not admissible to prove:
>
> - negligence;
> - culpable conduct;
> - a defect in a product or its design; or
> - a need for a warning or instruction.
>
> But the court may admit this evidence for another purpose, such as impeachment or—if disputed—proving ownership, control, or the feasibility of precautionary measures.

The purpose of Rule 407 is clear. If the design would not have been considered defective at the time the product was made, then hindsight cannot retrospectively make it defective.

On the other hand, evidence that the manufacturer had already decided to implement the remedial measures, but had not yet implemented that decision, is surely admissible, because that is not a matter of hindsight but of foresight. It goes to the heart of whether the instant product's design was defective or not.

Moreover, the Third Circuit held in *Diehl v. Blaw-Knox* that Rule 407 did not call for the exclusion of evidence of subsequent remedial measures taken by a non-party. As the court said, 360 F.3d 426, 430 (3d Cir. 2004), "it hardly makes sense to speak of a party's fault being 'admitted' by someone other than the party". The District Court's decision to exclude such evidence in that case was, therefore, reversible error.

It must also be emphasized that Rule 407 does permit evidence of a subsequent remedial measure to be admitted for the purpose of proving something other than product defect. In *Duchess v. Langston Corp.*, 769 A.2d 1131 (Pa. 2001), for example, the plaintiff, Mr. Duchess, had been injured while cleaning one of his employer's machines, which had been manufactured by the defendant, Langton. Duchess wished to introduce evidence of the subsequent fitting of an additional safety device, known as an interlock, to assist in his claim of a design defect. Because both the defendant's expert witness and counsel asserted that the alternative design proposed by the plaintiff was impractical, he was held to have been entitled to introduce evidence of subsequent remedial measures as a means of controverting that testimony.

7.7.1 State Law

Not all states have adopted the broad-brush approach of the federal courts. The Supreme Court of California observed in *Ault v. International Harvester Co.*, 13 Cal. 3d 113, 120 (1974):

> When the context is transformed from a typical negligence setting to the modern products liability field, however, the "public policy" assumptions justifying this evidentiary rule are no longer valid. The contemporary corporate mass producer of goods, the normal products liability defendant, manufactures tens of thousands of units of goods; it is manifestly unrealistic to suggest that such a producer will forego making improvements in its product, and risk innumerable additional lawsuits and the attendant adverse effect upon its public image, simply because

> evidence of adoption of such improvement may be admitted in an action founded on strict liability for recovery on an injury that preceded the improvement. In the products liability area, the exclusionary rule ... does not affect the primary conduct of the mass producer of goods, but serves merely as a shield against potential liability. In short, the purpose ... is not applicable to a strict liability case and hence its exclusionary rule should not be gratuitously extended to that field.

In other words, excluding evidence of subsequent remedial measures to prove fault is appropriate, but the same approach should not apply to the modern law of products liability. Several other states have taken a similar view to California. In *Forma Scientific, Inc. v. Biosera Inc.*, 960 P.2d 108 (Colo. 1998), for example, the Supreme Court of Colorado held that a manufacturer of ultra-cold freezers was strictly liable for a design defect after a freezer failed, causing the plaintiff's store of blood cell antibodies to be destroyed. Evidence of post-incident changes in the design of the freezers was held admissible because it helped to establish the appropriate level of expectations of the reasonable consumer (albeit that the "consumer" here was actually another business).

DESIGN DEFECTS CHECKPOINTS

- Depending on the jurisdiction, design defects may be determined by one or both of the following tests:
    - Consumer Expectations Test
    - Risk-Utility Test
- Within the risk-utility test, proof of a reasonable alternative design may be required, or it may be one of several factors involved.
- The reasonable alternative design requirement is inapplicable to prescription drugs and rarely applicable to medical devices.
- A product that was manufactured according to the state of the art at the time will not be considered to have a design defect.
- Remedial measures implemented after someone is injured cannot be used as evidence that the product design at the time was defective.

CHAPTER 8

Failures to Warn

FAILURES TO WARN ROADMAP

- Understand when there is a duty to warn
- Understand what a warning should say and where it should be placed
- Understand to whom a warning should be addressed

8.1 Reasonable Warnings

If a product works as intended, it will have neither a manufacturing nor a design defect. It might, nevertheless, present a danger to its users or consumers. A knife is a classic example; cars and power tools are others. For this reason, it is often appropriate for such products to come with usage instructions and warnings about what to check or avoid. When no such warnings are supplied, the product may suffer from a defect known as failure to warn.

In *Hardeman v. Monsanto Co.*, 997 F.3d 941 (9th Cir. 2021), for example, the Ninth Circuit affirmed a multi-million dollar judgment in favor of the plaintiff, who had contracted non-Hodgkin's lymphoma, because Monsanto had failed to warn users that the active ingredient in its product, Roundup, is carcinogenic.

Section 388 of the Second Restatement of Torts explains the obligation this way:

> One who supplies ... a chattel for another to use is subject to liability ... if the supplier
>
> (a) knows or has reason to know that the chattel is or is likely to be dangerous for the use for which it is supplied, and

> (b) has no reason to believe that those for whose use the chattel is supplied will realize its dangerous condition, and
>
> (c) fails to exercise reasonable care to inform them of its dangerous condition or of the facts which make it likely to be dangerous.

The main significance of this provision is that, while section 402A of the Second Restatement purports to apply the consumer expectations test to every type of product defect, section 388 clearly invokes a test of reasonableness.

Section 2(c) of the Products Liability Restatement achieves much the same effect, albeit while adopting rather different language:

> A product... is defective because of inadequate instructions or warnings when the foreseeable risks of harm posed by the product could have been reduced or avoided by the provision of reasonable instructions or warnings by the seller or other distributor, or a predecessor in the commercial chain of distribution, and the omission of the instructions or warnings renders the product not reasonably safe.

The point is that a warning needs to make the user reasonably safe. This implies, first, that it be sufficiently conspicuous to be noticed by a reasonable user or consumer. Second, it must specify the nature of the risks and their likely severity. And, third, it must provide the user with a reasonable way to manage, contain, or avoid those risks.

But this apparent agreement on the need for a test of reasonableness glosses over the ideological baggage that has led to the creation of two different methods for judging what reasonableness actually means. As explained in previous chapters, one is the consumer expectations test. The other is the risk-utility test, which effectively sets the standard as that of the reasonable manufacturer.

In either case, a warning should not be treated as a substitute for good design. If, for instance, a chainsaw needs a guard, it is not equally acceptable to warn of the need to take extra care because the design does not include a guard. That would still amount to a design defect.

8.1.1 The Sophisticated User

Significantly, however, neither Restatement requires a manufacturer to warn of an obvious risk. If a consumer is aware of the risk, no warning could convey any useful information. A knife, for example, is not required to have a label attached saying that it is sharp. That is, after all, why the consumer bought it.

But what if the user is more sophisticated than most users or consumers of the product? In *Johnson v. American Standard, Inc.*, 74 Cal. Rptr. 3d 108 (2008), the Supreme Court of California considered a complaint brought by a trained HVAC technician, who claimed that the maintenance and repairs he performed on air conditioning units in the normal course of his job created and exposed him to phosgene gas, causing him to develop pulmonary fibrosis. The court rejected his claim because he was a "sophisticated user" of the products involved and thus among those who should have been aware of these risks at the time of his injury.

8.2 A Duty to Warn?

Failure to warn claims are similar to claims of misrepresentation, so that there is often significant overlap between the two theories. There is, however, one significant difference. Misrepresentation concerns *mis*feasance. Except in a case of fraudulent concealment, the law typically takes the view that there is no duty to act. A failure to warn claim, by contrast, is essentially about *non*-feasance: it presupposes a duty to act. The fundamental question, therefore, is whether such a duty exists.

In *Geshke v. Crocs, Inc.*, 740 F.3d 74, 75 (1st Cir. 2014), the Court of Appeals for the First Circuit addressed an unusual claim about footwear:

> CROCS are odd looking shoes, known for their comfort. The plaintiff alleges that this reputation for comfort masks a hidden peril: the shoes present a heightened risk to the safety of wearers using escalators, and the manufacturer has failed to warn of this risk.

The court found, however, that the plaintiff had not provided any evidence to support the claim that CROCS posed a greater risk of injury on escalators than other shoes, and so there could be no duty to provide such a warning. Accordingly, summary judgment for the defendant was affirmed.

This decision highlights an important facet of failure-to-warn analysis. Because questions about the existence (or otherwise) of a legal obligation within the law of torts is always a matter of law, whether a duty to warn exists should normally also be a matter of law. In principle, therefore, it might be imagined that only if the judge rules that there was such a duty would a jury then be called upon to determine if the defendant had complied with the duty.

In practice, however, it is more complicated than that. The point is that there cannot be a duty to warn in the abstract. It must be a duty to say something specific. If the two issues were rigorously separated, it could lead to the absurd situation of a judge ruling that there was a duty to warn, only for the jury to say that no wording is possible to satisfy that duty.

8.2.1 What to Say?

Instead, any plaintiff claiming that there was a duty to warn must also both propose the text of such a warning and explain where it should have been displayed. Some products—for example, tobacco and pharmaceuticals—are already required as a matter of federal law to carry warnings whose wording is either specified or approved by a federal agency. For other products, the judge must determine if the plaintiff's arguments are sufficient to justify the imposition of a duty to warn. If not, the judge must order summary judgment for the defendant.

In *Mills v. Giant of Maryland, LLC*, 441 F. Supp. 2d 104 (D.D.C. 2006), for example, the plaintiffs claimed that the defendants had sold milk without proper warning labels. They suggested two possible labels:

> WARNING—IF YOU EXPERIENCE DIARRHEA OR STOMACH CRAMPS AFTER CONSUMING MILK, YOU MAY BE LACTOSE INTOLERANT. CHECK WITH YOUR PHYSICIAN.
>
> WARNING—LACTOSE INTOLERANT INDIVIDUALS MAY EXPERIENCE BLOATING, DIARRHEA, OR OTHER GASTROINTESTINAL DISCOMFORT FROM CONSUMING MILK. CHECK WITH YOUR PHYSICIAN.

The court rejected both. It noted that Comment *j* to the Second Restatement of Torts argued that a

> seller may reasonably assume that those with common allergies, as for example to eggs or strawberries, will be aware of them, and he is not required to warn against them.

The court also pointed out that, while lactose intolerance may cause discomfort, it is not a threat to life or limb. The low severity level of the potential harm did not warrant a duty to warn of the perils of ingesting lactose when drinking milk.

8.2.2 Where to Say It?

As *Mills* demonstrates, it must first be established what a warning might say before it is possible to decide whether there is indeed a duty to say it. But even if wording is established as appropriate in the circumstances, before there can be a duty to warn, it is still necessary to decide whether the defendant's burden of providing such information would be disproportionately high in comparison to the benefit of providing it.

This would not pose much of a problem in the case of sales of milk, since there is plenty of room on a milk carton to display a prominent warning. It could even be in a colored panel to make it stand out. But what if:

(a) The product, or its packaging, is too small to display a warning? or

(b) The product is so large that it would be difficult to know where to put the warning and be sure that it would be seen? or

(c) The product is used in an environment where any warning is likely to be quickly lost or abraded away? or

(d) The product is sold in bulk?

For (b), multiple warnings might be appropriate, though a common alternative is to supply an accompanying booklet or handbook. New cars and large home appliances, for example, typically come with a handbook, though a warning label might still be placed near to areas of particularly high danger.

A similar approach is typically taken with (c). Power tools, for example, often operate in very dusty environments that quickly wear away any warning labels, but they are typically supplied with a booklet explaining the dos and don'ts of operating the tool. The problem with this approach is that many users do not read the booklet, or forget where they put it, so that its contents effectively achieve little. For this reason, some manufacturers engrave warnings into a product, since these take much longer to be worn away.

So far as (d) is concerned, such products include things like sand and gravel. It is clearly impractical to attach a warning label to every grain or stone, and in most cases it simply makes no sense to supply such products in small packages. Instead, they are typically delivered by the truckload. Industry practice is that any relevant warnings are included in sales documentation or invoices, and even then normally only if there is an unusual hazard involved (such as the product containing more lime, or other allergenic ingredient, than is common). The courts have accepted this practice as satisfying the duty to warn.

8.3 Pharmaceuticals

As for (a), the most common example are pharmaceuticals. There is clearly no room to write a warning on a tablet, and the packaging or container is also typically too small to carry one. Instead, such drugs are typically packaged inside a box, whose main purpose is actually to enable a booklet—known as an insert—to be included that explains how the product is to be administered, when it is contra-indicated, and what potential side-effects there might be. From the point of view of the drug's manufacturer, this insert is absolutely critical.

As explained in Chapter 7, section 6(c) of the Products Liability Restatement makes it extremely hard to have a pharmaceutical manufacturer held liable for a design defect. This means that the main avenue for product defect claims against pharmaceutical manufacturers is failure to warn. It is, therefore, crucial that the insert contain all the relevant warnings to ensure that consumption of the drug will be reasonably safe.

8.3.1 Learned Intermediary

Where, however, a drug (or a medical device) is prescribed by a doctor, rather than being purchased over the counter, ensuring that the text of the insert is appropriate will not be sufficient for the manufacturer to avoid liability for a failure to warn. This is because, in such cases, it is important that the prescribing doctor be supplied with the correct information. Accordingly, section 6(d)(1) of the Products Liability Restatement provides that:

> A prescription drug or medical device is not reasonably safe due to inadequate instructions or warnings if reasonable instructions or warnings regarding foreseeable risks of harm are not provided to ... prescribing and other health-care providers who are in a position to reduce the risks of harm in accordance with the instructions or warnings....

The expectation is that the prescribing doctor will then pass on relevant warnings and instructions to the patient. This doctor then becomes what the law refers to as a "learned intermediary" between the product manufacturer and the patient. If the doctor fails to pass on appropriate warnings that were supplied by the manufacturer, then the latter will be effectively immune from suit, while the doctor will be liable for professional malpractice (i.e., negligence).

The learned intermediary also provides a shield to the liability of drug manufacturers in another respect. Many brand-name drugs that are available only on prescription are advertised to the general public. This means that, in order to obtain such drugs, a person must first consult a doctor. The law typically takes the view that a patient in such a case will *not* rely on the advertisement that made them seek out the doctor, on the grounds that that would be unreasonable since any representations made could only ever be generic. On the contrary, it considers the patient to have relied instead on the advice given by the prescribing doctor, who is in a much better position to provide an individual diagnosis and treatment regimen.

The main exception to this learned intermediary defense is where a manufacturer makes fraudulent misrepresentations, but manufacturers typically play it safe in any event by providing a long list of possible side-effects in their promotional materials.

8.4 The Heeding Presumption

In practice, of course, few patients read inserts, while users of many product do not pay attention to any warnings, irrespective of their source. Nevertheless, comment *j* to section 402A of the Second Restatement provides that the courts should apply a presumption that the warning would have been heeded. Most do so, but not all.

In *Rivera v. Philip Morris, Inc.*, 209 P.3d 271, 272 (Nev. 2009), for example, the Supreme Court of Nevada pointed out that the effect of the heeding presumption is to "shift[] the burden of proving the element of causation from the plaintiff to the manufacturer." It is then up to the jury to make the final determination of whether such a warning would have avoided or reduced the victim's injuries. The court chose to reject the presumption. Instead, it required plaintiffs to prove (a) that they would heeded the warning if it had been provided, and (b) that this would have meant either that they would have suffered less severely or that they would have avoided injury altogether.

8.5 Interaction with Other Products

The question of a duty to warn becomes harder to address when there is potential for it to interact with another product. In *Air and Liquid Systems Corp. v. DeVries*, 586 U.S. 446 (2019), Justice Kavanaugh observed in the US Supreme Court:

> [T]he federal and state courts have not reached consensus on how to apply that general tort-law "duty to warn" principle when the manufacturer's product requires later incorporation of a dangerous part in order for the integrated product to function as intended. Three approaches have emerged.
>
> The first approach is the more plaintiff-friendly foreseeability rule.... A manufacturer may be liable when it was foreseeable that the manufacturer's product would be used with another product or part, even if the manufacturer's product did not require use or incorporation of that other product or part.
>
> The second approach is the more defendant-friendly bare-metal defense.... If a manufacturer did not itself make, sell, or distribute the part or incorporate the part into the product, the manufacturer is not liable for harm caused by the integrated product—even if the product required incorporation of the part and the manufacturer knew that the integrated product was likely to be dangerous for its intended uses.
>
> The third approach falls between those two approaches. Under the third approach, foreseeability that the product may be used with another product or part that is likely to be dangerous is not enough to trigger a duty to warn. But a manufacturer does have a duty to warn when its product requires incorporation of a part and the manufacturer knows or has reason to know that the integrated product is likely to be dangerous for its intended uses. Under that approach, the manufacturer may be liable even when the manufacturer does not itself incorporate the required part into the product.

A majority concluded that the third approach is the most appropriate for maritime torts. While the dissent pointed out a number of "[h]eadscratchers," such as what counts as "incorporation" of the product, or as an "integrated product," those are endemic to the whole law of products liability, especially the economic loss rule.

Much more problematic is a situation where a defendant reasonably expects that the manufacturer of a third-party product will comply with its own duty to warn. Does that then absolve the defendant of responsibility, or should the defendant always take the pessimistic view that the third-party manufacturer will fail to provide the appropriate warnings? The law on these points remains unresolved.

8.6 Post-Sale Warnings

Also largely unresolved is the question of whether a new warning should be issued after a product is distributed because a latent defect has subsequently come to light. In the case of pharmaceuticals and medical devices, this is largely regulated by the Food and Drug Administration (FDA), which can order manufacturers to issue new warnings in addition to any that were provided when the product was originally sold, although manufacturers are able to add new warnings without prior authorization from the FDA if the seriousness of the new hazard requires it.

As far as other products are concerned, however, the states are split as to whether or not there is a duty to warn after the product has been sold. The Third Restatement acknowledges this difference of approach and thus confines itself, in section 10(b), to providing a list of factors for a court to consider in jurisdictions where a post-sale duty to warn is recognized:

1. the seller knows or reasonably should know that the product poses a substantial risk of harm to persons or property; and
2. those to whom a warning might be provided can be identified and can reasonably be assumed to be unaware of the risk of harm; and
3. a warning can be effectively communicated to and acted on by those to whom a warning might be provided; and
4. the risk of harm is sufficiently great to justify the burden of providing a warning.

8.7 Recalls and Retrofits

Recalls and retrofits go beyond post-sale warnings. They are appropriate when such a warning would likely be insufficient to keep a consumer safe. Since many jurisdictions are not prepared to impose a post-sale duty to warn, it should come as no surprise that the courts are even less keen to impose a duty to recall or retrofit unless there has been an order from the federal government.

The FDA may, for example, order the recall of contaminated processed food because there is likely no way for it to be eaten safely. With products not at risk of spoilage, an order to retrofit is more appropriate. This involves the seller regaining control of the product in order to make modifications to reduce the risk of harm. Cars are the product where retrofitting of a new or replacement part is most common.

FAILURES TO WARN CHECKPOINTS

- The duty to warn arises from what is reasonable, but this may be determined by either of the following tests, according to the jurisdiction:
  - Consumer Expectations Test
  - Risk-Utility Test
- If there is a duty to warn, the warning must:
  - Be conspicuous;
  - Inform the user of the risks and their likely severity; and
  - Provide a reasonable means for the user to manage, contain, or avoid the risks.
- The test of reasonableness is modified for two specific types of users:
  - The sophisticated user
  - The learned intermediary
- Some jurisdictions operate a heeding presumption.
- The states have adopted divergent views on whether a product manufacturer should warn about possible risks arising from that product interacting with other products.

CHAPTER 9

Causation

CAUSATION ROADMAP

- Understand what the law recognizes as harm
- Understand the difference between general and specific causation
- Understand the gatekeeping role of judges
- Understand the basic methodology of epidemiology and Bradford Hill's evidentiary factors
- Understand the special rules applicable to asbestos cases

9.1 Harm

As previous chapters have explained, product liability claims fall into six broad categories:

- Breach of warranty
- Misrepresentation
- Negligence
- Manufacturing defect
- Design defect
- Failure to warn

Each of these contains its own sub-types. Yet all of them share one common characteristic. In each case, one of the elements to be proved is that the defect in question was a cause of the victim's injuries.

Causation cannot occur in the abstract. It must lead to harm. Products liability law requires in nearly every case that the initial harm be physical rather than economic or emotional. Both personal injury and property damage are considered to be physical harm, and so both are potentially compensable.

Three additional points are also worth noting at this stage. The first is that economic loss and psychological harm that results from such physical harm are also compensable. So, while pure economic losses (including harm to the product itself) and emotional distress that does not result from physical injury are not recognized as compensable harms by products liability law, both the loss of an income and psychological trauma that result from a physical injury are so recognized.

9.1.1 Enhanced Injuries

Secondly, as section 16(a) of the Third Restatement of Torts: Products Liability makes clear, even if some harm would have been sustained by the victim without there being any defect in the product at hand, any "increas[e in] the plaintiff's harm beyond that which would have resulted from other causes" is also a form of recognized harm.

In *Bensenberg v. FCA US LLC*, 31 F.4th 529 (7th Cir. 2022), for example, the Court of Appeals for the Seventh Circuit held that a car manufacturer cannot escape responsibility for a defective airbag on the grounds that the accident in which the victim was injured was primarily caused by a medical episode suffered by the driver. The purpose of the airbag is to keep injuries in such circumstances to a minimum so that, if the airbag fails to deploy above a threshold speed, the manufacturer can be held liable for the victim's enhanced injuries caused by the failure to deploy.

9.1.2 Latent Diseases and Medical Monitoring

Thirdly, an individual may become aware of having been exposed to a toxic substance—such as a carcinogen—but be unable to make a claim for physical injury at that point because the diseases with which that toxic agent is associated have long latency periods. The question is whether that means that such a person has to wait until such harm manifests itself, by which point relevant evidence may have been lost or destroyed and relevant witness may have died or be otherwise impossible to locate.

Some courts have been prepared to ameliorate this situation by recognizing a claim for the expenses of appropriate medical monitoring. In *Hansen v. Mountain Fuel Supply Co.*, 858 P.2d 970 (Utah 1993), a case concerning exposure to asbestos, the Supreme Court of Utah laid out a set of eight requirements for such a claim to succeed:

1. Exposure
2. to a toxic substance,
3. which exposure was caused by the defendant's negligence,
4. resulting in an increased risk
5. of a serious disease, illness, or injury
6. for which a medical test for early detection exists
7. and for which early detection is beneficial, meaning that a treatment exists that can alter the course of the illness,
8. and which test has been prescribed by a qualified physician according to contemporary scientific principles.

The Supreme Court of Louisiana adopted a similar checklist in *Bourgeois v. A.P. Green Indus., Inc.*, 716 So. 2d 355 (La. 1998), but the Louisiana legislature subsequently passed legislation to prevent awards for medical monitoring in future cases. Many other states have also rejected the idea of claims being made for medical monitoring. Such a rejection is based on the view that such a claim is best characterized either:

(a) as one of pure economic loss (i.e., payment for the medical monitoring), which is precluded by the economic loss rule; or

(b) as one for the fear of suffering some dreadful disease in the future, which is also precluded because, without any manifestation of physical harm, it is simply a form of pure emotional distress.

9.2 Causation in Fact

Only if the alleged harm sustained is legally recognized can a case then move on to consider causation. It is often said that this doctrine is divided into two elements, namely (a) cause in fact and (b) proximate causation. The truth is, however, that tort law is rather more complex, and this is particularly true in products liability cases.

9.2.1 Proximate Cause vs Scope of the Risk

The Third Restatement of Torts: Liability for Physical and Emotional Harm makes it clear that the terminology of "proximate causation" should be abandoned because it is misleading. "Proximate" is misleading because the plaintiff does not actually have to prove that the causative agent was in any way close; while "causation" is misleading because what is at stake in this context is not whether the causative agent caused the harm—that is a matter for cause in fact—but whether the harm sustained by the victim was of a foreseeable type.

Instead of such confusing terminology, the Restatement favors the term "scope of the risk," because it more accurately captures what is involved. The type of foreseeable harm is what sets the "scope" of the risk involved. Not every jurisdiction has yet adopted this terminology, but doing so helps to avoid misconceptions about what is involved. So, whether this specific label has been adopted in any given jurisdiction or not, the substance of the law of causation is that it is subdivided into (a) cause in fact and (b) scope of the risk.

An issue of rather more significance concerns cause in fact. While often overlooked in a 1L Torts class, this doctrine itself actually has two distinct elements, and the plaintiff must satisfy both of them in order to establish a *prima facie* case. These elements are known as "general causation" and "specific causation."

9.3 General Causation

General causation requires that the plaintiff prove, on a preponderance of the evidence, that the allegedly defective product is *capable* of causing the *type* of injury alleged. Specific causation, by contrast, requires the plaintiff to show that the product in question *actually did cause* the plaintiff's injuries.

In a "garden variety" products liability case, such as that involving an allegedly defective vehicle, everyone already knows that car accidents are capable of causing a variety of physical and emotional injuries, so proof of general causation is simply assumed. Indeed, this may also be true of some other products liability cases (as would be the case if the car wreck had allegedly been caused by a defective tire). In such a case, there would again be no need to prove general causation.

The position is, however, different when dealing with claims concerning products about which knowledge is limited. These involve products that are new—often pharmaceuticals or medical devices—or that allegedly contain latent defects whose effects became apparent only after some time has elapsed. In such cases, the plaintiff must prove that the product in question is capable of causing the type of injury sustained. In other words, they must prove general causation.

Note that what is at stake here is proof that the defect could cause a particular *type* of harm. There is no need to prove the likely *extent* of harm, since the usual tort rule applies that a defendant must take the victim as they find them. If the victim happens to be more susceptible to serious injury—for example, a moderate wound becomes life-threatening because the victim has a blood clotting disorder—that is irrelevant so far as proof of general causation is concerned.

9.3.1 Judge vs Jury

If general causation cannot be proved, the plaintiff's case fails and the case never moves onto specific causation. It might be objected that, if the plaintiff can prove that the product did actually harm them—i.e., *specific* causation—then it must follow that the product is capable of causing such harm—i.e., *general* causation—and so there should be no need to prove general causation independently in such cases.

But this objection misses the point. The doctrine of causation in fact is not bifurcated for reasons of logic. The purpose of bifurcation is to allocate the two different questions to two different decision-makers.

General causation requires a generic or systemic finding on whether a given product is capable of causing injuries of a particular type. This means that it is an issue of law for the court, which makes it particularly amenable to summary judgment. In many cases, general causation presents the biggest hurdle of all the issues that the plaintiff has to overcome. This is because it typically requires recognition that the product is capable of causing this type of harm when such a result has never been recognized before. Yet, as just noted, if general causation cannot be proved, the plaintiff's case fails and the case never moves onto specific causation.

This is the real significance of the independent requirement to prove general causation. It enables the trial judge to act as gatekeeper by preventing cases that are not supported by credible expert evidence from ever reaching the jury. Only if the judge decides that there is sufficient evidence to support a theory of general causation will the jury then be charged with deciding the question of specific causation, which is concerned with evaluating the evidence about the specific case at hand.

9.3.2 General Causation vs Scope of the Risk

If the judge considers that a theory of general causation is sufficiently supported by the evidence, then the case goes to the jury to determine specific causation. If the jury finds for the plaintiff on this point, however, the law finds itself in an uncomfortable spot. For the jury must now address scope of the risk.

This asks whether the type of harm caused was of a foreseeable type. Yet, when deciding general causation, the judge asked whether the product defect was capable of causing the type of harm. In principle, therefore, it is possible to have the judge determine that the defect was capable of causing the type of harm sustained, while the jury finds that the type of harm sustained was not foreseeable. While this might logically make sense, it is likely that judge and jury will both effectively be trying to answer much the same question.

This raises the question of whether having a judge decide the question of general causation means effectively usurping the role of the jury. It is particularly problematic if an appellate court rules out general causation before there has been sufficient time to carry out the testing and research to provide reliable evidence either way, since this will bind all future trial courts without there ever being a proper evidential hearing. That risks precipitating what has been called an "accountability crisis."

9.3.3 Uncertainty, Probability, and Inference

It must be emphasized that the plaintiff is not expected to provide 100% proof of any aspect of causation. By definition, the preponderance of the evidence standard requires only that the plaintiff establish that their theory of each element of the case is more than 50% likely to be true.

This means that, for all the talk of causation, what the judge (for general causation) and jury (for specific causation and scope of the risk) are really being asked to adjudicate upon is the *degree of probability* that the alleged product defect caused the victim's injuries.

However, unless the probability is clearly either 100% (certain to have caused the harm) or zero (certain *not* to have caused the harm), it is difficult to know how great a probability should be assigned to causation. Moreover, in order to generate relevant statistics on which to base their claims of probability about what no-one knows for certain, expert witnesses inevitably draw *inferences* based on experience and testing of what is known.

Yet without some agreed basis for assigning specific degrees of probability to each event, such numbers will essentially be meaningless. Much of that agreed basis is provided by the field of epidemiology.

9.3.4 Epidemiology

In 1854, a cholera epidemic broke out in the Soho district of London, England. There had been several previous such epidemics in England since 1849, and they had killed tens of thousands of people. But they seemed to come to an end as mysteriously as they began, and no-one had been able to determine the cause.

Dr. John Snow, who had already become a leader in the field of surgical anesthesia, talked to those who knew the victims of the 1854 outbreak to establish where they had lived, worked, and gone to school, and where they had obtained their drinking water. He plotted the results on a map and inferred that the cause was water drawn from a specific public pump. The handle of the pump was promptly removed, and the epidemic came to an end very shortly afterwards. Snow had not identified the precise cause of the cholera, but he had correctly inferred that it is a water-borne disease.

Snow is now seen as the founding father of epidemiology. So-called because it was originally concerned with identifying the causes of epidemics, it has now become one of the foremost methods of identifying causes of any new disease. Accordingly, it is heavily relied on in so-called "toxic tort" cases. Indeed, by 1990, the Court of Appeals for the Third Circuit was able to observe, *DeLuca v. Merrell Dow Pharmaceuticals, Inc.*, 911 F.2d 941, 954 (3d Cir. 1990):

> The reliability of expert testimony founded on reasoning from epidemiological data is generally a fit subject for judicial notice; epidemiology is a well-established branch of science and medicine, and epidemiological evidence has been accepted in numerous cases.

For our purposes, epidemiology is primarily concerned with the question of general, rather than specific, causation because, 911 F. 2d 941, 945 (1990), "[e]pidemiological studies do not provide direct evidence that a particular plaintiff was injured by exposure to a substance." Instead, epidemiology invites the drawing of inferences from a strong association between a potential causative agent and a particular type of harm. Such associations arise, just as in Snow's analysis of a cholera outbreak, from the identification of patterns or distributions of disease that seem unlikely to be the product of mere chance.

If no such pattern or distribution can be identified in a toxic tort case, then a court will almost certainly rule that the plaintiff has failed to establish general causation, and will dismiss the case. Where such a pattern or distribution is identifiable, then the second role of epidemiologists is to attempt to identify the likely causal factors, and thus to rule in or rule out as a potential cause the product that is the focus of the litigation.

Epidemiological evidence does, however, have inherent limitations. The circumstances cannot ethically be reproduced for a random trial, for example, and we may even lack sufficient scientific knowledge to make plausible sense of the findings. These limitations mean that those carrying out such studies must be especially careful to choose a representative sample of cases and to develop their explanatory theory according to accepted norms of scientific reasoning.

9.3.5 Evidence of Causation

It was not until 1965 that such norms were set out in a manner that met general approval. Sir Austin Bradford Hill was an English epidemiologist and statistician who pioneered the randomized clinical trial. In 1950, he and a colleague had been the first to demonstrate the connection between cigarette smoking and lung cancer. Fifteen years later he suggested, *The Environment and Disease: Association or Causation?* 58 Proc. Royal Soc'y Med. 295 (1965), that the following nine factors should be taken into account in assessing evidence of causation:

- *Chronology:* This is the only necessary factor. The symptom identified must occur after exposure to the potential causative agent.
- *Strength of Association:* The higher the relative risk, the greater the likelihood that the relationship between agent and symptom is causal.
- *Dose-Response Relationship:* Greater exposure to the agent usually (but not always) leads to greater incidence of the symptom.
- *Degree of Replication:* The higher the degree of replication, the more likely it is that there is a causal relationship between agent and symptom.

- *Plausibility:* If a scientifically plausible explanation for a potential causal mechanism can be provided, it strengthens the credibility of the argument that there is such a mechanism.
- *Coherence:* Laboratory experiments may be able to support a theory or rule out alternative possibilities.
- *Real-Life Experiment:* Removing real-life exposure to the agent may provide new evidence to support or undermine a causative relationship, although the condition of those already impacted may continue to get worse in any event.
- *Specificity:* The more specific an association between a factor and a symptom, the greater the probability of a causal relationship.
- *Analogy, or Consistency with Other Relevant Knowledge*: Similarity to a known pattern of causation associated with a similar product strengthens the likelihood that the product in question was a cause of the victim's harm.

It is worth noting that each of these factors involves drawing an inference, and that inference may be wrong. In the medical community, it is, therefore, considered important that the factors be considered together as a whole rather than individually.

While Bradford Hill was writing for a scientific audience, the courts have universally adopted this checklist of factors when assessing whether general causation has been established through epidemiology. In a multidistrict product liability action concerning the drug Abilify, for example, the US District Court for the Northern District of Florida ruled, in *In re Abilify (Aripiprazole) Products Liability Litigation*, 299 F. Supp. 3d 1291 (N.D. Fla. 2018), that epidemiological evidence presented by the plaintiffs was sufficient to make it arguable before a jury that Abilify could cause impulsive and irrepressible urges to engage in certain harmful behaviors, including impulsive gambling, eating, shopping, and sex.

The courts have, however, tended to place greater weight on the dose-response relationship and the degree of replication than the medical community does. They do so on the grounds that these tests are more objectively verifiable and less prone to subjective interpretation by individual experts than all the other tests except chronology.

9.3.6 Asbestos

The law on asbestos-related harms is a case study in the courts' use of epidemiology. While much remains unknown about the causal mechanisms by which humans contract asbestosis (a severe, chronic lung disease that is not fatal) and mesothelioma (a form of lung cancer that is always terminal), epidemiological evidence has shown conclusively that these two diseases can be contracted only as a result of exposure to asbestos.

Accordingly, in a case where the victim has contracted one of these diseases, there is no longer any issue of general causation to be satisfied. All causes other than asbestos can be ruled out; the question centers instead solely on a matter of cause in fact, which is whether the source of the victim's exposure was the allegedly defective product at the heart of the litigation.

9.4 Specific Causation

If the plaintiff fails to establish general causation, the case will be dismissed on summary judgment or by way of a directed verdict. If they succeed in establishing that there is sufficient evidence to support a contention of general causation, they must then go on to prove specific causation. In other words, the plaintiff must prove *both* general causation *and* specific causation. While general causation is a matter for the judge, specific causation is a matter for the jury.

Specific causation requires that the plaintiff establish that the product in question actually caused the injuries they suffered. There are currently three tests that may be employed to establish specific causation, although not all of them are recognized in every jurisdiction:

1. The "but-for" test;
2. The "substantial factor" test; and
3. The "contribution to the risk" test.

9.4.1 But-For Test

Traditionally, the law of torts has claimed to rely on the but-for test to determine questions of causation in fact. It requires that the plaintiff prove, on a preponderance of the evidence, that they would not have been injured (or, at least, not so severely) but for the product's defect.

Unfortunately, this test suffers from three fundamental problems. The first two may be considered together. These are that the test requires that the plaintiff prove both:

- A negative: that they would not have been injured; and
- A counter-factual: that something would have happened but did not actually happen.

It is clearly impossible to prove either requirement directly. Instead, the plaintiff must satisfy both elements by drawing inferences from the evidence. The plaintiff has essentially to paint a picture of a hypothetical scenario where every factor is identical to what actually took place except for one modification: the product is not defective. So, for example, the car's brakes work, or the power tool has a guard in place. The jury is then invited to consider what would have happened in such circumstances.

If the jury concludes that the injury would not have occurred (or, at least, not with the same degree of severity), then that creates a strong implication that the defect in the product was the cause of the plaintiff's injuries.

The problem is that such inferences are not always easy to draw. Say, for example, that the car with the problematic brakes was being driven on an icy road. How is the jury to know whether properly-functioning brakes would have stopped it before it hit the victim? In such cases, it is as well to remember that the law does not require certainty for "proof" to exist. Just as in every other element of the case, the plaintiff needs to establish their case only on a preponderance of the evidence. This means that "proof" of a but-for cause means simply that the plaintiff's theory is more than 50% likely to be true.

But that leaves us with the third difficulty inherent in the but-for test. It is this: if the circumstances suggest that the victim's injuries were caused by more than one factor operating at the same time, the but-for test will actually conclude that none of them was a cause! This is because, if a hypothetical is created as above with a specific product defect removed from the equation, the injury would still occur because of the remaining causative agents.

This means that the but-for test cannot be used in circumstances where there is allegedly more than one cause. Of course, that in itself puts the cart before the horse, since it means determining whether there is more than one cause before deciding whether to apply the but-for test, which is supposedly designed to determine cause!

9.4.2 Substantial Factor Test

This absurdity has meant that the law has come to recognize an alternative test for causation. Known as the "substantial factor" test, it been expressly adopted by section 16(a) of the Products Liability Restatement:

> When a product is defective at the time of commercial sale or other distribution and the defect is a substantial factor in increasing the plaintiff's harm beyond that which would have resulted from other causes, the product seller is subject to liability for the increased harm.

One difference between this and the but-for test is that, while the latter seeks to identify *the* cause of the victim's injury, the former is interested only in ensuring that the defective product in question was *a* cause of the victim's harm. As recognized in, for example, *Roemmich v. 3M Company*, 509 P.3d 306 (Wash. Ct. App. 2022), it is thus capable of being applied in circumstances where there might have been more than one operative cause.

Moreover, this test does not require either proof of a negative or of a counter-factual. It does still typically require the jury to infer causation, but such inferences are to be drawn from what actually happened rather than from what did not.

Nevertheless, a word of warning is in order for this test too. Usage of the word "substantial" in this test is unfortunate. It is not meant to imply that the defective product must have been a "large" factor, and certainly not the "main" factor. What "substantial" means in this context is simply that the defective product played a role "of substance" in causing the victim's injury. In other words, it played a part that was more than negligible. It is for the jury to determine what degree of significance is required in order to be substantial.

9.4.3 Contribution to the Risk Test

The "contribution to the risk" test was first articulated in a judgment of the House of Lords in the United Kingdom, where Lord Reid said, in *McGhee v. National Coal Board*, [1973] 1 W.L.R. 1, 5:

> I can see no substantial difference between saying that what the [defendants] did materially increased the risk of injury to the [plaintiff] and saying that what the [defendants] did made a material contribution to his injury.

Although this might seem like an obvious logical fallacy, it is important to remember that the doctrine of causation—and its subdivisions—is not founded on logic, but on a desire to dispense practical justice. Lord Reid himself argued that he was taking "a broad and practical viewpoint." Thus, in his view, if the plaintiff can establish on a preponderance of the evidence both

(a) that they have suffered harm, and

(b) that the defendant materially increased—i.e., contributed to—the risk of that harm,

it then makes practical sense to infer that the defendant made a material contribution to—i.e., was a cause of—the plaintiff's injury.

While a prevailing notion of "American exceptionalism" has made it hard for courts to cite a modern case from overseas, courts throughout the US have clearly adopted such an approach, albeit that some have folded it into the "substantial factor" test.

Cases involving asbestos are classic examples of the application of the contribution to the risk test. Where a defect in a defendant's product caused someone to be exposed to asbestos fibers, and that person subsequently contracted either asbestosis or mesothelioma, the fact that their risk of contracting those diseases was materially increased by the defendant's product creates an inference that the defective product was indeed a cause of the victim's harm.

9.4.4 Market Share Liability

None of the above tests adequately addresses the question of what to do when the defective product responsible for causing the victim's injury is known, but several different organizations manufactured and sold that product, and it is impossible to know *whose* product caused the harm. In such circumstances, whatever answer is provided to the question of specific causation must be the result of either guesswork or stipulation.

Where the product in question is truly fungible (which rules out asbestos-related claims, since there are several different types of asbestos), a minority of states have adopted a theory of "market share liability." This holds as liable every business that distributed the defective product at the time, but with each one paying a fraction of the victim's total compensation in proportion to their respective market share.

9.4.5 Reading and Heeding Warnings

Failures to warn present a unique causation problem. At their heart, such cases are about proving that the failure to provide a warning was a cause of the victim's injuries. Yet it is hard for a victim to prove that they would have (a) read and (b) heeded any warning provided, since that amounts to proving something that did not happen.

Chapter 8 pointed out that some states adopt a "heeding presumption," which means that the court presumes that the victim would have paid attention to such a warning, so that the failure to provide one is thus presumed to be a cause of the victim's injuries. This puts the burden of proof on the defendant to show that the absence of a warning would have made no difference.

Crowston v. Goodyear Tire & Rubber Company, 521 N.W.2d 401 (N.D. 1994), provides an example of where a defendant managed to do just that. It called a psychiatrist, who offered his expert opinion that the victim had an anti-social personality disorder which made it highly unlikely he would have read or followed any additional warnings, but would instead act on his own internal impulses and do the opposite of directions or warnings.

More recently, in *Hubbard v. Bayer Healthcare Pharmaceuticals, Inc.*, 983 F.3d 1223, 1225 (11th Cir. 2020), the Court of Appeals for the Eleventh Circuit addressed the issue after Karen Hubbard had suffered a catastrophic stroke:

> The stroke left her paralyzed and her cognitive functions severely impaired. Her oral contraceptive, Beyaz—a drug known to increase the risk of blood clots that can cause strokes—may have been to blame.... Georgia's learned intermediary doctrine ... imposes on prescription drug manufacturers a duty to adequately warn physicians, rather than patients, of the risks their products pose. But a plaintiff claiming a manufacturer's warning was inadequate bears the burden of establishing that

an improved warning would have caused her doctor not to prescribe her the drug in question. The Hubbards have not met this burden. The prescribing physician testified unambiguously that even with the benefit of the most up-to-date risk information about Beyaz, he considers his decision to prescribe Beyaz to Karen Hubbard to be sound and appropriate. Under our binding precedent interpreting Georgia law, the Hubbards, therefore, cannot recover. Though the Hubbards have suffered greatly, the law plainly entitles Bayer to summary judgment.

CAUSATION CHECKPOINTS

- Harm must be physical (i.e., personal or proprietary), except in states where claims for medical monitoring are recognized.
- General causation is a matter of law for a judge to rule on whether the product defect is capable of causing the type of harm alleged.
- General causation in toxic torts claims relies heavily on epidemiological evidence, which involves the drawing of inferences from the following factors:
  - Chronology
  - Strength of Association
  - Dose-Response Relationship
  - Degree of Replication
  - Plausibility
  - Coherence
  - Real-Life Experiment
  - Specificity
  - Analogy, or Consistency with Other Relevant Knowledge
- Specific causation is a matter of fact for the jury to decide whether:
  - The harm sustained was actually caused by the product defect; and
  - The injuries sustained by the victim were of a reasonably foreseeable type.

- Specific causation involves the application of one or more of the following tests:
    - But-For Test
    - Substantial Factor Test
    - Contribution to the Risk Test
- In cases of failure to warn, causation in fact requires that the question be addressed of whether the victim would have read and heeded the warning.

CHAPTER 10

Expert Evidence

EXPERT EVIDENCE ROADMAP

- Understand the role of an expert
- Understand who qualifies as an expert
- Understand the rules governing the admissibility of expert evidence
- Understand the gatekeeping role of judges

10.1 A Question of Weight or Admissibility?

Chapter 9 explained how experts will typically be required to opine on matters of general causation. In fact, they will also often have a role to play in assisting the court on matters of specific causation too. But their role goes much further, for they will also typically be called upon to assist on questions of product design (including the feasibility of alternative designs) and even, in some cases, on the feasibility of the provision of warnings.

Experts occupy a privileged position in a law court. Although they do not have the power to make findings of law or fact, their opinions will carry significant weight with both judge and jury. Indeed, if a case involves a product about which the judge or jury know very little, they will essentially be forced to adopt either the views of the plaintiff's expert or those of the defendant's expert; they will be in no position to reach a wholly independent view.

Moreover, experts are the only witnesses permitted—indeed, they are often encouraged—to speculate about what might have happened in a hypothetical that differs from the facts of the case at hand. Since several legal tests require proof of a negative or a counter-factual, the judge and jury will inevitably need such guidance in order to arrive at a rational conclusion that is supported by the evidence.

Many products liability cases are, accordingly, won or lost on the quality of the expert evidence provided by each side. But that begs an even more fundamental question, namely whether the evidence provided by the expert will even be admitted by the court. If the judge rules that one party's proffered witness is not an expert, that party's apparent expert evidence will have no-one to vouch for it, and so it will be inadmissible. It is, therefore, critical for each side to ensure that they choose their experts carefully.

10.2 Probative or Prejudicial?

As Judge E. Grady Jolly put it in *Viterbo v. Dow Chemical Co.*, 826 F.2d 420, 422 (5th Cir. 1987):

> As a general rule, questions relating to the bases and sources of an expert's opinion affect the weight to be assigned that opinion rather than its admissibility and should be left for the jury's consideration. In some cases, however, the source upon which an expert's opinion relies is of such little weight that the jury should not be permitted to receive that opinion.... Furthermore, its lack of reliable support may render it more prejudicial than probative, making it inadmissible under Fed. R. Evid. 403.

The rule of evidence to which Judge Jolly referred says:

> The court may exclude relevant evidence if its probative value is substantially outweighed by a danger of one or more of the following: unfair prejudice, confusing the issues, misleading the jury, undue delay, wasting time, or needlessly presenting cumulative evidence.

10.3 The *Frye* Test

Unfortunately, there is a conflict among the jurisdictions about the proper standard to apply in evaluating whether someone should be admitted as an expert. The original approach was based on a criminal law case, *Frye v. United States*, 293 F. 1013 (1923), where a defense expert claimed to be able to use his own "lie detector" machine to distinguish truthful answers from false ones by measuring the respondent's blood pressure. The Court of Appeals set out the test of admissibility in these terms:

> [W]hile courts will go a long way in admitting expert testimony deduced from a well-recognized scientific principle or discovery, the thing from which the deduction is made must be sufficiently established to have gained general acceptance in the particular field in which it belongs.

Applying this test, the *Frye* court found that:

> [T]he systolic blood pressure deception test has not yet gained such standing and scientific recognition among physiological and psychological authorities as would justify the courts in admitting expert testimony....

10.4 The *Daubert* Test

Widespread adoption of the *Frye* test provided a means for the courts to prevent parties calling upon self-proclaimed experts to expound fanciful theories. At the same time, however, the test inevitably favored views of long-standing over those that reflected more recent testing and research. This drawback was highlighted seventy years later in *Daubert v. Dow Merrell Pharmaceuticals,* 509 U.S. 579 (1993), before the US Supreme Court.

The petitioners in *Daubert* were minor children born with serious birth defects. They and their parents sued *Dow Merrell*, alleging that the birth defects had been caused by the mothers' ingestion of Dow's prescription antinausea drug, Bendectin. Dow's expert stated that he had reviewed all the literature on Bendectin and human birth defects: a total of more than 30 published studies involving over 130,000 patients. No study had found Bendectin to be capable of causing malformations in fetuses. On the basis of this review, the trial judge had granted Dow's motion for summary judgment on general causation.

The petitioners appealed and sought to have their own expert testimony admitted in evidence. Based upon "in vitro" (test tube) and "in vivo" (live) animal studies that found a link between Bendectin and malformations; pharmacological studies of the chemical structure of Bendectin that purported to show similarities between the structure of the drug and that of other substances known to cause birth defects; and the "reanalysis" of previously published epidemiological (human statistical) studies, eight experts argued that Bendectin was, indeed, capable of causing birth defects.

The petitioner's experts had been ruled inadmissible at trial (and this had been affirmed on appeal) because the court had concluded that the evidence which they were proffering was not, as required by the *Frye* test, "sufficiently established to have general acceptance in the field to which it belongs" because it had not been published or subjected to peer review.

By a majority, the Supreme Court reversed. Ironically, it did not do so for substantive reasons but because it held that the *Frye* test had been superseded by the adoption of the Federal Rules of Evidence, specifically Rule 702. The Court noted, 509 U.S. 579, 588–89 (1993), that: "Nothing in the text of this Rule establishes 'general acceptance' as an absolute prerequisite to admissibility." Instead, a "trial judge must ensure that any and all scientific testimony or evidence admitted is not only relevant, but reliable."

Peer review and publication is a factor to be taken into account in deciding whether the evidence is admissible, but the lack of it is not an absolute bar. Indeed, as the Court recognized, 509 U.S. 579, 593 (1993), "Some propositions, moreover, are too particular, too new, or of too limited interest to be published." On the other hand, 509 U.S. 579, 594 (1993):

> Widespread acceptance can be an important factor in ruling particular evidence admissible, and "a known technique which has been able to attract only minimal support within the community" may properly be viewed with skepticism. (Citation omitted.)

Kumho Tire Co. v. Carmichael, 526 U.S. 137, 141 (1999), subsequently extended the reach of *Daubert* beyond "scientific" knowledge to include also testimony based on "technical" and "other specialized" knowledge. Rule 702 was accordingly revised in 2000 to take account of both judgments, and then again in December 2023, so that it now reads:

> A witness who is qualified as an expert by knowledge, skill, experience, training, or education may testify in the form of an opinion or otherwise

if the proponent demonstrates to the court that it is more likely than not that:

(a) the expert's scientific, technical, or other specialized knowledge will help the trier of fact to understand the evidence or to determine a fact in issue;

(b) the testimony is based on sufficient facts or data;

(c) the testimony is the product of reliable principles and methods; and

(d) the expert's opinion reflects a reliable application of the principles and methods to the facts of the case.

10.5 Judge vs Jury Revisited

In his dissent in *Daubert*, Chief Justice Rehnquist argued, 509 U.S. 579, 594 (1993), that this confuses relevance with reliability. It is certainly part of the judge's role to ensure that only relevant evidence is heard by the jury, but it is surely the jury's role to determine reliability. Only if the supposedly expert evidence is so unreliable as to be irrelevant should the judge take the decision to rule it inadmissible.

The majority accepted this was a risk but, 509 U.S. 579, 596–97 (1993), considered it a risk worth taking to enable the practical resolution of lawsuits:

> [T]here are important differences between the quest for truth in the courtroom and the quest for truth in the laboratory. Scientific conclusions are subject to perpetual revision. Law, on the other hand, must resolve disputes finally and quickly.... We recognize that, in practice, a gatekeeping role for the judge, no matter how flexible, inevitably on occasion will prevent the jury from learning of authentic insights and innovations. That, nevertheless, is the balance that is struck by Rules of Evidence designed not for the exhaustive search for cosmic understanding but for the particularized resolution of legal disputes.

In practice, however, a judge will be unable to assess the four factors in Rule 702 without hearing the evidence that the expert will give (especially under cross examination). This typically leads courts to hold a so-called "*Daubert* hearing" without the jury present before the trial "proper". Then the judge can decide whether the allegedly expert testimony should be admitted. If so, such evidence will have to be presented twice: once to the judge alone in a *Daubert* hearing and then again in front of the jury.

Where the medical community generally recognizes the toxicity of the drug or chemical at issue—as with toxins like asbestos and cigarettes—there will be no need for a *Daubert* hearing on the question of general causation, though there might still be a need for such a hearing on specific causation. Where, however, the medical community does not generally recognize the agent as capable of causing the injury that the plaintiff alleges, a *Daubert* hearing may be necessary to assess expert evidence on both issues.

10.6 *Frye* vs *Daubert* in State Courts

Since *Erie Railroad v. Tompkins*, 304 U.S. 64 (1938), there has been no such thing as a federal common law of torts. Ever since, the law of torts has, therefore, been principally a matter for the states, while the law of contracts for the sale of goods has always been recognized as within the province of the states. Yet, by definition, the Federal Rules of Evidence apply only to the federal courts. It is, therefore, important to know what approach the states take to the admissibility of expert evidence.

They are, in fact, divided about whether—and how—to apply *Frye* or *Daubert*. While the majority have now adopted something close to the *Daubert* approach, it is often with limitations and caveats. It is also worth emphasizing that, if a case is removed to federal court by reason of diversity jurisdiction, it will be subject to the *Daubert* test and Rule 702 even if the state whose substantive law is to be applied uses the *Frye* test in its own courts.

Moreover, the battle between the *Frye* and *Daubert* tests soon became highly politicized, probably because it occurred at much the same time that the controversy between the Second and Third Restatement of Torts was raging. *Frye* was supported by those who favored the Second Restatement, which is generally seen as more favorable to plaintiffs. *Daubert* was supported by those who favored the Products Liability Restatement, which is generally seen as favorable to defendants.

This picking of sides was somewhat ironic, because the decision in *Daubert* itself was favorable to the plaintiffs, who had no realistic prospect of success under the *Frye* test. Yet the *Frye* supporters soon had their worst fears confirmed about *Daubert* when the Supreme Court ruled, just four years later, in *General Electric Co. v. Joiner*, 522 U.S. 136 (1997), that the standard by which an appellate court should review a trial court's decision to admit or exclude expert testimony under *Daubert is* abuse of discretion.

10.7 Judge as Gatekeeper

This means that a judge's "gatekeeping" decisions to admit or reject expert testimony can be overturned on appeal only if they have acted unreasonably. Since reasonable people can disagree, this in turn means that there is no guarantee of consistency. But if all that *Daubert* achieves is to replace unpredictable jury verdicts with unpredictable decisions by trial judges, then it is legitimate to ask what is the point.

Indeed, empirical evidence suggests that *Daubert, Joiner, and Kumho Tire* have really changed very little about the way that state courts deal with the admissibility of expert evidence. This is one of the motivations behind the most recent updates to Rule 702 in December 2023. The revised Rule now makes clear that the proponent of expert testimony has the burden of satisfying the judge by a preponderance of the evidence—i.e., that it is more likely than not—that each each of requirements (a) to (d) are met. It also limits the degree of speculation that is permitted from an expert witness by requiring that any opinions expressed "reflect[] a reliable application of the principles and methods to the facts of the case."

These updates to Rule 702 highlight the judge's responsibility as gatekeeper, allowing into evidence only what is both germane and reliable. In *McClain v. Metabolife International, Inc.*, 401 F.3d 1233 (11th Cir. 2005), by contrast, the trial judge had protested:

> Trying to cope in this case without a pharmacological, or a medical, or a chemical, or a scientific background, the court cannot fully and fairly appreciate and evaluate the methodology employed by either of these witnesses as they reached the conclusions they reached, conclusions that a jury could not reach without some expert opinion testimony. Neither can the court fully appreciate or evaluate the criticisms made by defendant of the proposed testimony of these witnesses, especially when the criticisms do not come from competing proposed experts. This court does not pretend to know enough to formulate a logical basis for a preclusionary order that would necessarily find, as a matter of law, that

these witnesses cannot express to a jury the opinions they articulated to the court.

The Court of Appeals for the Eleventh Circuit held that this was an abdication of responsibility and thus a form of abuse of discretion.

A *Daubert* hearing should not, however, be thought of as a way to improperly shortcut the process. In a class action, for example, it will not normally be appropriate to have the court rule on the admissibility of expert witnesses at trial when the court has yet to decide whether to certify the class in the first place: "There is less need for the gatekeeper to keep the gate when the gatekeeper is keeping the gate only for himself." *United States v. Brown*, 415 F.3d 1257, 1269 (11th Cir. 2005).

EXPERT EVIDENCE CHECKPOINTS

- There is a split among the states about the test for admissibility of expert evidence. The majority and the federal system favor the *Daubert* test and Rule 702 of the Federal Rules of Evidence. These require that expert testimony must be evaluated by the trial judge to ensure, on a preponderance of the evidence, that:
    - (a) the expert's scientific, technical, or other specialized knowledge will help the trier of fact to understand the evidence or to determine a fact in issue;
    - (b) the testimony is based on sufficient facts or data;
    - (c) the testimony is the product of reliable principles and methods; and
    - (d) the expert's opinion reflects a reliable application of the principles and methods to the facts of the case.
- A minority of jurisdictions continue to favor the *Frye* test, which asks whether the evidence presented is generally accepted in the particular field to which it belongs.

CHAPTER 11

Affirmative Defenses

AFFIRMATIVE DEFENSES ROADMAP

- Understand the difference between an affirmative defense and a denial of the plaintiff's *prima facie* case
- Understand the gatekeeping role of judges
- Understand the different types of defenses

11.1 Types of Defenses

A defendant may defeat a products liability claim in two ways. They might successfully deny one of the elements of the theory of the case that the plaintiff is seeking to prove. Alternatively, they might successfully argue that, *despite* the plaintiff proving every element of their theory of the case, there is still a legitimate reason why the defendant should escape liability.

This distinction does not merely dictate the point at which the issue is considered. It also dictates which party has the burden of producing the relevant evidence. In the first group of cases, that burden lies squarely on the plaintiff; in the latter group, it is on the defendant. For this reason, the latter category is said to comprise *affirmative* defenses: they must be affirmatively supported by evidence introduced by the defendant. They are the subject of this chapter.

Note that this means that the defendant will nearly always be better served by seeking, if possible, to deny an element of the plaintiff's *prima facie* case. Once that is established, it creates a rebuttable presumption that the plaintiff is entitled to a remedy, and so the defendant is then at a disadvantage. A successful affirmative defense rebuts that presumption, but it amounts essentially to a fallback position to be relied on only when denial of the plaintiff's *prima facie* case has failed.

The distinction between denying an element of the plaintiff's *prima facie* case and denying liability *despite* the plaintiff's *prima facie* case is not, therefore, merely semantic. The only circumstances where it would be advantageous to emphasize an affirmative defense are those where the evidence to support it is so clear that a judge could be persuaded to rule on it as a matter of summary judgment.

Affirmative defenses typically available to a defendant in a products liability case may broadly be divided into three groups:

1. Defenses based on the victim's own conduct;
2. Defenses based on a contract between the defendant and the government; and
3. Defenses based on the lapse of time.

11.1.1 Justification or Excuse?

Another way to categorize defenses is according to whether they are justifications or excuses. An excuse means that, while the defendant did something wrong, the law has decided to excuse that behavior. A classic example is where the plaintiff waited too long before bringing a lawsuit.

A justification, on the other hand, means that the defendant did nothing wrong in the first place. This would be the case when a patient suffers a recognized side-effect from taking a widely-prescribed drug. If the drug was prescribed and administered for the very condition for which it was intended, and the patient was given the appropriate warning, then there was no wrongdoing of any kind by the manufacturer.

Note, however, that justifications like this are typically better argued as denials of the plaintiff's primary case. There are thus no grounds for a failure to warn claim in this example because the appropriate warning was provided.

11.2 Defenses Based on the Victim's Own Conduct

Affirmative defenses that are based on the victim's own conduct are often said to be consent, assumption of risk, contributory negligence, comparative fault, comparative causation, and failure to mitigate. But this list is apt to confuse. In particular, consent and assumption of risk are not quite what they might appear to be.

11.2.1 Consent

Consent is a defense only to cases of potentially *intentional* torts. Injecting or force-feeding someone without their consent would be a battery; if consent is given, it is no longer a tort at all. This is often expressed in the Latinism, *volenti non fit injuria*, which means "to one who consents, there can be no injury."

In fact, however, the defendant would do better to argue the point as a denial of an element of the victim's *prima facie* case. This is true of almost every products liability case where consent is given. Yet manufacturers and distributors do not typically create defective designs with the intention of harming the users of their products; nor does any deviation from a reasonable design typically occur because the manufacturer or distributor was deliberately trying to harm someone.

In cases of misrepresentation or failure to warn, an intent to harm is more likely. Yet any harm intended will almost always be purely economic, which is not a form of harm usually recognized by products liability law. Moreover, it is impossible to consent to such defects. If the plaintiff "consents" to being misled, they are not actually being misled at all.

Finally, no sane person consents to negligence. A medical equipment manufacturer whose oxygen cylinders are used by an anesthetist in an operating room for a procedure to which the plaintiff has consented is still liable for negligence if they filled one of those tanks with nitrous oxide instead of oxygen.

So it turns out that there is, in effect, no defense of consent in products liability cases. The defense of consent applies to the type of conduct in which the defendant engaged, not to the type or extent of any injury caused by that conduct. The point is that the types of conduct in which defendants engage in products liability cases are almost never behaviors to which the plaintiff could consent. As in the hypothetical above, any apparent instance of a "defense" of consent in a products liability cases almost certainly involves a mislabeling; it will almost always be better characterized as a denial of an element of the plaintiff's *prima facie* case.

11.2.2 Assumption of Risk

Assumption of risk is another apparent affirmative defense that turns out, in practice, to be no such thing. One source of confusion about this particular doctrine is that it is often known as "*voluntary* assumption of risk," which causes it to be confused with consent. Yet, in fact, assumption of risk comes in two flavors: express and implied.

While express (or primary) assumption of risk is established when someone signs a waiver or disclaimer, implied (or secondary) assumption of risk does not require any conscious consideration of the matter by the plaintiff, and is simply "deemed" by the law to have been present. Deeming that a person assumed a risk is nothing like the same thing as a finding that the person voluntarily consented to it.

11.2.2.1 Express Assumption of Risk

But even express assumption of risk is a highly problematic defense, because it typically has no role to play in products liability law. It is worth recalling, for example, that the federal Magnuson Moss Warranty Act provides, 15 U.S.C. § 2308(a), that if an express warranty is supplied, the implied warranty of merchantability (and, if applicable, the implied warranty of fitness for a particular purpose) cannot be excluded. Moreover, the combined effect of sections 2-302, 2-316, and 2-719 of the UCC is to make apparent agreements that limit claims for personal injury *prima facie* unenforceable.

Similarly, the courts regard waivers and disclaimers of liability for manufacturing and design defects as contrary to the very policy that led to creation of products liability law. If waivers and disclaimers were permitted, manufacturers and distributors would have little incentive to make their products safer.

So far as negligence is concerned, just as no sane person consents to it, no sane person agrees to the risk of its occurrence. The real legal significance of the medical waivers and disclaimers that patients are routinely asked to sign is to create a record of the patient having been *told* of certain risks. In other words, the paperwork provides a means of denying a claim of a failure to warn or of a misrepresentation by showing that an accurate warning was provided.

What it emphatically does *not* do is provide the patient's assent to negligent treatment. Express assumption of risk is no more a defense to a products liability claim than consent.

11.2.2.2 Implied Assumption of Risk

Implied assumption of risk is said to occur when a plaintiff knew of a risk and chose to run it anyway. But this too is misleading. It is simply incoherent. Drivers of cars all know of the risks of using the highway, yet those who tortiously injure them are not relieved of liability on the basis that the victim knew of the risks they were running.

Similarly, if a woman decides to have an IUD fitted, her consent to the medical procedure will provide the nurse, midwife, or OBGYN with a defense to conduct that would otherwise amount to the intentional tort of battery. If, before reaching her decision, she was appropriately informed about the risks inherent in such a procedure, even if carried out correctly and with a fully-functional device, then it might be said that she has assumed the risk of one of those things happening.

But she has clearly not assumed the risk of the IUD being defective. If the IUD is defective, then the manufacturer will be liable.

Moreover, the patient's apparent assumption of the inherent risks of an appropriate procedure is again not really a defense. It is more accurately characterized as a denial of an essential element of a claim of a failure to warn. Since she was given the appropriate warning, there is no basis for a failure to warn claim and therefore no need for any affirmative defense at all.

11.2.3 Contributory Negligence

Contributory negligence involves a situation where the victim's own unreasonable behavior contributed in some way to their own injuries. This typically involves misusing the product, such as using it for a purpose or in a manner for which it was not intended.

Unlike consent and assumption of risk, it is a genuine affirmative defense. It is, however, confined to the law of torts. It is, therefore, inapplicable to claims of breach of warranty. It is also typically inapplicable to cases of intentional wrongdoing, because that level of fault is so egregious that there is no good reason for permitting a lower level of fault, like negligence, to reduce the defendant's liability.

Even within the rest of the law of torts, however, it is significantly confined. It does not apply to cases of manufacturing defects because, like breaches of warranty, those are matters of strict liability. Notions of negligence are out of place in that context.

Design defects are a more problematic category. According to one reading of section 402A of the Second Restatement of Torts, such defects are—like manufacturing defects—also concerned with strict liability. In jurisdictions that adopt that approach, the defense of contributory negligence is again inapplicable.

On a reading of section 402A that emphasizes the need to show "unreasonable danger," however, design defects involve a form of negligence. This is also, without question, the view adopted by the Products Liability Restatement. In jurisdictions that take either of these views, the defense of contributory negligence is potentially available. It is also available in both negligence and failure to warn cases.

The effect of a successful defense of contributory negligence is that the plaintiff loses. Even a small degree of negligent behavior on the part of the plaintiff means that their whole case is lost, and they will receive nothing. Most jurisdictions have, however, taken the view that this is too drastic a consequence, so that only Alabama, Maryland, North Carolina, Virginia, and the District of Columbia continue to retain it.

11.2.4 Comparative Fault

In every other US jurisdiction, contributory negligence has been replaced by the defense of comparative fault (although, confusingly, some jurisdictions continue to use the old label for the new defense). A successful plea of comparative fault means that the amount to be paid for the plaintiff's injury must, in principle, be apportioned between the parties according to their respective degrees of fault.

A complicating factor is that, while this is how a so-called "pure" scheme works, only a minority of states have adopted such a scheme. The clear majority have instead adopted a type of "modified" scheme. These impose a threshold requirement, according to which the defendant must be found to have been—depending on the jurisdiction—at least 50%, or more than 50%, to blame for the victim's injuries in order for the plaintiff to receive anything. The Products Liability Restatement has not attempted to standardize the approach.

Comparative fault is also applicable where more than one defendant has contributed to the victim's injuries. Historically, those defendants would have been regarded as being jointly and severally liable, where each defendant is liable for 100% of the victim's injuries. However, a clear majority of states have abolished joint liability (except in cases of vicarious liability), so that liability is also now more typically apportioned among defendants according to the degree of their respective fault.

The general acceptance of comparative fault is another reason why courts have rejected notions of assumption of risk as an affirmative defense. Recognition of assumption of risk would enable the resuscitation of the plaintiff's conduct as a complete bar to recovery. It would thus render the defense of comparative fault redundant. If a defense argument cannot be framed as a denial of an element of the plaintiff's *prima facie* case, so that it might then be tempting for a defendant to plead assumption of risk as an affirmative defense, it should typically be pleaded instead as an instance of comparative fault.

11.2.5 Comparative Causation

The problem with comparative fault (irrespective of whether it involves apportionment of liability between defendants or between plaintiff and defendants) is that it often requires a comparison between two (or more) incomparable behaviors. The defendant's fault will typically lie in its manufacture or design of a product, or in failing to warn about a significant danger. The fault of the victim will typically involve them either misusing the product or in engaging in some other unreasonable behavior unrelated to the product itself.

There is clearly no objective standard by which to measure the respective degrees of fault involved. Instead, the law simply relies on the jury to come up with a rough-and-ready set of percentages that sound like they bear some sort of connection to the evidence. Although it is often said that the role of the jury is to determine matters of fact, this is really more a matter of collective judgment.

A more objective approach, therefore, has considerable appeal. That is what comparative causation offers. Instead of dividing up the financial responsibility for the victim's injuries according to respective degrees of fault, comparative causation makes each party liable for the amount of harm they caused: nothing more, nothing less.

It is possible that applying comparative causation will lead to the same result as comparative fault, but that result is not very common. Take the example of a motorist who is driving too fast and careens off a bend in the road. Braking hard, the car nevertheless hits a tree and the car's airbags automatically deploy. But the airbags are faulty and shower her with debris, as if she has just been hit by shrapnel. When the paramedics arrive to cut her free, she looks like she has been the victim of a small bomb.

Applying comparative fault, a jury would have to weigh the degree of the motorist in driving too fast against the degree of fault by the manufacturer in creating a product with either a manufacturing or design defect. The extent of the motorist's injuries will be irrelevant to this calculation. Only once the respective percentages have been determined will they then be applied to see how much each party should pay towards the victim's compensation.

Applying comparative causation would involve a completely different approach. This would ask what the motorist's injuries would have been if the airbags had deployed safely. Those costs would then have to be borne by the victim herself, since it was her negligence that caused them. The manufacturer would then be liable for all the harm caused by the defective airbags.

As this example demonstrates, the real advantage of comparative causation is that it uses the traditional doctrine of causation to apportion liability. While this does, as explained in Chapter 9, involve a need to prove a hypothetical that did not happen, this problem is likely to be easily resolved because the injuries caused by the motorist's negligence are almost certainly very different in kind from those caused by the defective airbags. It should not, therefore, be very hard for the jury to determine who should be responsible for what.

Unfortunately, comparative causation is not always available. If the hypothetical is modified so that, instead of defective airbags (which now deploy safely), the car had defective brakes, the problem should become apparent. Now *both* the motorist's negligence *and* the car's defect caused the initial crash. That means that the injuries sustained by the victim are indivisible. Both causes contributed to the same injury, and it is impossible to attribute specific injuries to only one specific cause. When an indivisible injury occurs, comparative causation cannot be applied; comparative fault (or contributory negligence) must be applied instead.

11.2.6 Comparative Fault as a Sword, Not a Shield

Florida has seen a novel development in the law of comparative fault. Litigation against cigarette manufacturers had been dragging on for decades, when plaintiffs' attorneys started to adopt a new tactic. They pleaded that their own clients were comparatively at fault. In other words, they sought to show that the defendant manufacturers were liable, but that they should be relieved of a proportion (normally around one third) of the plaintiff's compensation claim.

This might seem absurd, since it means that, if their client wins, they will receive significantly less than would have been the case if comparative fault had not been pleaded. But the purpose behind this approach is to make it much more likely that their client will win. A jury now sees not a greedy money-grubber who seeks to blame anyone but himself, but instead a reasonable human being who is taking responsibility for their own bad decisions. That almost inevitably make the jury members ask themselves: "Why should the manufacturer not also take its share of responsibility?"

This strategy was heavily vindicated. When manufacturers then denied any responsibility, juries consistently took such a dim view that they awarded not only the percentage of compensatory damages requested but also significant punitive damages.

It remains to be seen whether courts in other jurisdictions will permit plaintiffs to plead comparative fault.

11.2.7 Failure to Mitigate

Once a victim has sustained injury caused by a defective product, the harm should not be allowed to fester. The victim must instead act reasonably to mitigate the harm. That means taking appropriate steps to keep the harm to a minimum. The cost of them doing so will have to be borne by the defendant, since it is in the defendant's interest to limit the harm.

Someone who cuts themselves on an exposed blade that should have been shielded, for example, should keep the wound clean and seek appropriate medical treatment. If a tetanus shot is then prescribed but the victim refuses to have one, or if the victim simply fails to seek medical advice, the manufacturer cannot then be held liable for any harm beyond the original wound. If the victim goes on to contract tetanus, the victim will have to bear that burden themselves.

On the other hand, if the victim in this scenario did take the tetanus shot but suffered an unforeseeable allergic reaction (so that the doctor could not have been at fault), the manufacturer *would* be liable for this added complication. It was the manufacturer's defective product that put the victim in the position of having to seek medical treatment and, since that treatment was reasonable, it is the manufacturer who should pay both for it and its consequences.

11.3 Government Contractors

It is well known that, at common law, the government used to enjoy the complete defense of sovereign immunity when faced with claims for compensation for committing a tort or a breach of contract. The Tucker Act of 1887 abrogated this immunity for claims of breach of contract. The Federal Tort Claims Acts of 1946 and 1948 purported to do much the same for many types of torts, but not for torts arising out of the exercise of "a discretionary function or duty."

States too enjoyed sovereign immunity at common law, although most of them have now also passed legislation analogous to the Federal Tort Claims Acts. Yet such legislation has proved of relatively little effect because state courts have tended to follow the direction of the U.S. Supreme Court in *Feres v. U.S.*, 340 U.S. 135 (1950), which significantly limited the ambit of the Federal Torts Claims legislation. Since *Feres*, sovereign immunity has effectively expanded.

All this might seem irrelevant to cases of products liability. After all, while government may commission major infrastructure projects, it does not itself manufacture or distribute products. In fact, however, the courts have often been prepared not just to expand the range of tortious conduct for which they will grant the government immunity; they have also extended sovereign immunity to cover contractors working for the government. These contractors are, therefore, often said to enjoy "derivative sovereign immunity."

11.3.1 Military Contractors

In *Boyle v. United Technologies Corp.*, 487 U.S. 500 (1988), a United States Marine helicopter copilot was killed when the helicopter in which he was flying crashed during a training exercise. His father sued the contractor responsible on the basis of a design defect in the helicopter and won at trial. The Supreme Court held, 487 U.S. 500, 505 (1988), however, that:

> The present case involves an independent contractor performing its obligation under a procurement contract, rather than an official performing his duty as a federal employee, but there is obviously implicated the same interest in getting the Government's work done.

This remarkable elision of the distinction between employee and independent contractor was apparently justified because, 487 U.S. 500, 507 (1988):

The imposition of liability on Government contractors will directly affect the terms of Government contracts: either the contractor will decline to manufacture the design specified by the Government, or it will raise its price. Either way, the interests of the United States will be directly affected.

The Court then went on to say, 487 U.S. 500, 511 (1988):

We think that the selection of the appropriate design for military equipment to be used by our Armed Forces is assuredly a discretionary function within the meaning of [the Federal Torts Claims Act] ...

Liability for design defects in military equipment cannot be imposed ... when

(1) the United States approved reasonably precise specifications;

(2) the equipment conformed to those specifications; and

(3) the supplier warned the United States about the dangers in the use of the equipment that were known to the supplier but not to the United States.

Accordingly, judgment was rendered for the defendant manufacturer.

11.3.2 Non-Military Contractors

While the government contractor defense has sometimes been called the "military contractor" defense, this label is something of a misnomer. Some courts have also been prepared to hold that manufacturers of products that are designed, built, and used solely for civilian purposes are entitled to avail themselves of the defense.

In *Carley v. Wheeled Coach*, 991 F.2d 1117 (3d Cir. 1993), for example, the Court of Appeals for the Third Circuit addressed an appeal against the grant of summary judgment dismissing a claim for personal injuries caused by an alleged defect in an ambulance manufactured by defendant Wheeled Coach. A majority of the court noted that the distinction between employee and independent contractor had been treated as insignificant in *Boyle*. It also noted that:

[T]he imposition of liability on an independent contractor who enters into a procurement contract with the United States directly implicates the significant federal interest in the completion of the government's work. That significant federal interest exists regardless of whether the procurement contract is military or nonmilitary in nature.

Accordingly, it held that the government contractor defense is also available to non-military contractors. That settled the design defect claim. But the court remanded the case to the district court on the question of failure to warn because that claim had not been properly addressed. It ruled that, if Wheeled Coach "failed to prove that it warned the United States government of dangers in its ambulance known to Wheeled Coach but not to the government," it would reverse the grant of summary judgment and remand for trial.

Subsequent case law has seen immunity from liability for a design defect given to the manufacturer of a postal service vehicle and to construction companies engaged in the performance of federal public works and infrastructure projects.

11.3.3 Applicability to Types of Defect

As these case demonstrate, immunity from liability for design defects will be available where the government approves reasonably precise specifications and the product in question conformed to those specifications. There need not be explicit approval of every detail of the design; the point "is that the contractor cannot have been delegated all discretionary design decisions and reap the benefit of the immunity defense." *Sewell v. Sewerage and Water Board of New Orleans*, 697 Fed. Appx. 288, 292 (5th Cir. 2017).

Immunity from claims of a failure to warn is also available, but only if the contractor warned the government about the hazards associated with use of the product that were known to the contractor but not to the government. While the government exercises discretion in approving a design, it does not mean that the government considered the appropriate warnings, if any, that should accompany the product. These often involve balancing many different considerations, which might not have been apparent at the time when the design was approved.

Federal law thus makes it possible for a government contractor to be immunized against liability for design defects and failures to warn. But it does not provide immunity for manufacturing defects. The latter occur when the product either (according to the Second Restatement of Torts) does not meet consumer expectations or (according to the Third Restatement) differs from the intended design. There is no reason to immunize a contractor for a defect that establishes that the product was not in accordance with government expectations, and nor can it be said that an unintended defect is the result of the exercise of discretion.

In general, the states have tended to track federal law on this issue. Moreover, if a defendant in an action in state court was acting as a contractor to the federal government, the doctrine of pre-emption—discussed in greater length in Chapter 12—may apply, so that federal law will govern the case in any event.

One wrinkle that the Ninth Circuit Court of Appeals has been especially keen to emphasize is that government contractors enjoy immunity from *liability*, not immunity from suit altogether. *Rodriguez v. Lockheed Martin Corp.*, 627 F.3d 1259 (9th Cir. 2010). On this basis, the court has signaled strongly that summary judgment for government contractors on the grounds of this immunity is inappropriate. Instead, trials should be allowed to proceed so that the strength of evidence led in support of the plea of derivative sovereign immunity can be tested.

11.4 Defenses Based on Lapse of Time

The third group of affirmative defenses are those based on the lapse of time, after which a victim may be barred from seeking compensation. Such lapses of time involve statutes of limitation and statutes of repose.

11.4.1 Statutes of Limitation

As in every other branch of the civil law, victims of alleged product defects must bring their claims in a timely fashion. This provides a degree of predictability to potential defendants, who would otherwise be open to lawsuits in perpetuity. Statutes of limitation are the traditional means of imposing time limits on the bringing of such suits. They require that a plaintiff bring suit within a specified time limit after the tort or breach of warranty has occurred.

Each jurisdiction has its own statute of limitations, and so the precise periods specified differ from one jurisdiction to the next. Typical limitation periods for claims brought in the law of torts are one or two years. Typical limitation periods for breach of warranty contracts claims tend to be longer: the default rule in section 2-725 of the UCC specifies four years. The differing periods obviously have a bearing on which types of products liability claims may be successfully pursued once a certain amount of time has elapsed.

11.4.1.1 Conflicting Limitation Periods

One problem is that it is sometimes unclear which jurisdiction's statute of limitations should prevail. Section 142 of the Restatement (Second) of Conflicts of Law sets out how this issue will normally be resolved. If the forum state has a substantial interest in the litigation brought in its courts, then that state's statute of limitations will normally apply. If, on the other hand, the forum state has no such "substantial interest"" in the claim, it should then, according to section 6(2), consider the following factors:

1. The needs of the interstate and international systems,
2. The relevant policies of the forum,
3. The relevant policies of other interested states and the relative interests of those states in the determination of the particular issue,
4. The protection of justified expectations,
5. The basic policies underlying the particular field of law,
6. Certainty, predictability and uniformity of result, and
7. Ease in the determination and application of the law to be applied.

On the other hand, it is sometimes possible that two different limitation periods *from within the same jurisdiction* apparently apply to the same case. Thus a particular jurisdiction may have one limitation period for a certain type of injury and a different limitation period for a specific type of claim. If that claim and that type of injury are implicated together, both limitation periods cannot apply. Courts will instead typically apply whichever is the shorter period.

11.4.1.2 Tolling

A particular problem with many toxic torts cases is that the victim will often be in no position to realize that they have been harmed until after the limitation period has apparently expired. In such cases, the statute of limitations is said to be "tolled," by a "discovery rule," so that time is treated as effectively standing still until the plaintiff becomes aware, or should have become aware, of the injury.

Similarly, statutes of limitation are tolled for injuries suffered by children and the mentally incompetent until the former reach the age of majority or the latter regain mental acuity. They are also tolled if the defendant unlawfully conceals evidence of responsibility for the victim's injury, until such time as the latter becomes aware (or should have become aware) of the relevant information.

In cases where there is repeated or continual exposure to a defective product (such as would occur when inhaling toxic fibers or gases), the limitation period is continually re-started to run from the time of the latest exposure. But sometimes such exposure can lead to different types of injury manifesting themselves at different times. In *Pooshs v. Philip Morris USA, Inc.*, 51 Cal. 4th 788 (2011), the plaintiff was diagnosed first with chronic obstructive pulmonary disease (COPD), then with periodontal disease, and later with lung cancer. On each occasion, she knew that smoking was the cause, but she did not sue the manufacturer of the brand to which she had become addicted until she received the cancer diagnosis.

The Supreme Court of California noted that the plaintiff's COPD involved the same part of the body (the lungs) as her lung cancer. But, on the basis that COPD is a separate illness, which does not pre-dispose or lead to lung cancer, it held that to be irrelevant for the purposes of the discovery rule. By the time of the litigation, a lawsuit for the COPD would have been barred by the statute of limitations. But the plaintiff's awareness of the COPD had not triggered the statute of limitations for a lawsuit based on the cancer, which could accordingly proceed.

11.4.2 Statutes of Repose

Product manufacturers and distributors have been among the most vocal supporters of so-called "tort reform." Statutes of limitation have been one of the areas of law said to be in need of reform. The tolling of limitation periods has been particularly criticized, since that means that it is hard to know whether a particular threat of litigation has passed. This problem can, however, be overcome by statutes of repose, which have thus come become symbols of tort reform alongside the Products Liability Restatement and the *Daubert* case.

One of the hallmarks of the tort reform movement is that it seeks to move decision-making away from the jury and leave it instead in the hands of the judge. The replacement in the Products Liability Restatement of the consumer expectations test with the risk-utility test is a classic example, as are the changing rules of evidence on admissibility of expert evidence, which give judges more power and often result in cases being resolved at summary judgment.

Statutes of repose involve a similar approach. They operate by providing a defendant with a complete defense after the expiry of a specific period of time, which cannot be tolled unless the defendant unlawfully conceals evidence of its responsibility for the victim's injury.

Moreover, unlike statutes of limitation, where the relevant period of time begins at the point of the commission of a tort or breach of warranty, the point at which the clock starts to tick for statutes of repose has little to do with the facts of a specific case. Instead, the clock starts at the time when the product was manufactured, sold, delivered, or first used. It typically expires between four and twelve years later.

While interpreting its statute of repose, Georgia's Court of Appeals ruled, *L'Oreal USA, Inc. v. Burroughs*, 903 S.E.2d 740 (Ga. 2024), that the statute's reference to the the "first sale" of a product refers to the sale of the first unit of repeatedly purchased products. Subsequent sales do not then re-start the period of repose as they would for a limitation period.

As a result, plaintiffs who suffer an injury may find that they are unable to bring a claim because the time period which their state has deemed appropriate for such claims has already passed. This is particularly troublesome for plaintiffs who have contracted a devastating disease with a long latency period, such as lung cancer or mesothelioma.

Where a statute of repose conflicts with a statute of limitations, the courts will apply the legislation whose period expires first. If a tort or breach of warranty is immediately apparent, the relevant limitation period will usually (though not always) expire first. Where, however, the injury has a significant latency period, it will almost always be the repose period that is the first to expire.

11.4.2.1 Constitutionality

Many statutes of repose have been challenged as unconstitutional on the grounds that they remove or eliminate the rights of victims of defective products without allowing those victims a jury trial. Many of those challenges were initially successful. In the last decade or two, however, the courts have become much more reluctant to rule that a statute of repose is unconstitutional on its face. As-applied challenges do, nevertheless, succeed with a certain degree of regularity.

The reason for the change of perspective is essentially as follows. The courts have clearly signaled what the minimum length of repose periods should be, and legislatures have come into compliance. This has, in turn, allowed the courts to draw an analogy with statutes of limitation, which have long been regarded as constitutional, and then hold that statutes of repose are also facially constitutional.

Yet an as-applied challenge to the constitutionality of a statute of repose may still succeed. In *Groch v. Gen. Motors Corp.*, 883 N.E.2d 377 (Ohio 2008), for example, the Supreme Court of Ohio was faced with a case where the plaintiff was seriously injured by an allegedly defective press just 34 days before the repose period was due to elapse. The Court noted that the relevant limitation period in Ohio was two years and then held that 34 days was an unreasonably short period in which to expect a victim to file a lawsuit. Accordingly, the state's statute of repose was unconstitutional for the purposes of Groch's case.

The court emphasized, however, that if Groch had actually been injured 35 days later, he would have been left entirely without a remedy. That is because his right to compensation would never have vested before the statute of repose applied.

In other words, provided that the period of repose specified in the legislation is not unreasonably short, there is nothing unconstitutional about preventing a victim from gaining a right to sue at all. If, however, a victim does acquire such a right, a statute of repose cannot have the effect of taking it away within an unreasonably short period.

AFFIRMATIVE DEFENSES CHECKPOINTS

- Because of the difference in the evidential burden, attempting to deny the plaintiff's *prima facie* case is always a better approach for a defendant than relying on an affirmative defense, unless the affirmative defense is supported by such clear evidence that it forms the basis for summary judgment.
- Consent and assumption of risk are best characterized as denying an element of the plaintiff's *prima facie* case.
- There are three types of affirmative defenses:
    - Defenses based on the victim's own conduct;
    - Defenses involving a contracts between the defendant and the government; and
    - Defenses based on the lapse of time.

- Defenses based on the victim's own conduct are:
  - Contributory negligence;
  - Comparative fault;
  - Comparative causation; and
  - Failure to mitigate.
- Government contractors may also enjoy immunity for design defects and failures to warn.
- Defenses based on the lapse of time involve:
  - Statutes of limitation; and
  - Statutes of repose.

CHAPTER 12

Role of Federal Law

ROLE OF FEDERAL LAW ROADMAP

- Understand the difference types of pre-emption
- Understand the basic requirements for multi-district litigation and class actions
- Understand the significance of a defendant entering into bankruptcy protection

12.1 Pre-Emption

In *Erie Railroad Co. v. Tomkins*, 304 U.S. 64 (1938), the US Supreme Court ruled that there is no such thing as a federal common law of torts. This means that, when a torts case is tried in federal court, the substantive tort law to be applied is not federal law but the law of the state most relevant to the case at hand. (The Federal Rules of Civil Procedure will, however, continue to apply.)

Federal statutes are a different matter. Under the Supremacy Clause of the US Constitution, "Laws of the United States ... made in Pursuance" of the Constitution are "the supreme Law of the Land; and the Judges in every State shall be bound thereby." This means that if federal legislation—or, under the Necessary and Proper Clause, a federal agency acting under powers granted by federal legislation—purports to lay down the law within an area authorized by the Constitution, then that law prevails over any state law with which it is in conflict.

In other words, state law will be overridden (or, as it is more commonly expressed, "pre-empted") when Congress has passed a statute which conflicts with state law in an area within the competence of the federal government. So far as products liability is concerned, that competence is dictated by the Commerce Clause, which governs the regulation of "Commerce with foreign Nations, and among the several States, and with the Indian Tribes."

In order to decide whether state products liability law is pre-empted in any given case, a test involving three questions is applied:

1. Is there a federal law that has some bearing on the instant case?
2. If so, does that federal law purport to regulate interstate commerce?
3. If so, is there a conflict between that federal law and the relevant state law?

If the answer to *any* of these questions is "No," then the federal law can safely be ignored and the case can proceed on the basis of state law in the usual manner. But if the answer to *all three* questions is "Yes," then the state law in question is effectively rendered null and void, and the lawsuit will be dismissed.

12.1.1 Conflicts

So far, so good. Indeed, the first two questions rarely present much of a problem. But there is significant controversy about how to know when there is a conflict between federal law and state law. No-one doubts that an express provision in the federal statute that declares that it pre-empts state law achieves exactly what it says. The converse is also true; if a federal law declares that it does not pre-empt state law, then that statement will also be honored by the courts.

The difficulties arise when there is no such declaration either way. In other words, the problem is knowing when state law has been *impliedly* pre-empted. One such type of case will potentially arise when a federal law permits product manufacturers and distributors to exercise an element of discretion in the design or manufacture of the product in question. But conflict will then exist only if all of the following conditions are met:

- The federal law provides options from which manufacturers and distributors may choose;
- The same law also makes clear that the regulated parties must remain free to choose among those options; and
- The defendant complied with one of the permitted alternatives.

If all those conditions are met, then a state law that purports to specify a particular standard that is different from the one chosen by the defendant will clearly conflict with the federal law, because it will have the effect of eliminating any discretion.

Similarly, if a product that falls within the remit of the Consumer Product Safety Commission (CPSC) develops an issue that might otherwise generate a post-sale duty to warn or a recall, any such potential duty will be pre-empted. This is because the CPSC has, under powers granted to it by the Consumer Product Safety Act (CPSA) of 1972, promulgated regulations that dictate specifically how such warnings or recalls should be handled.

Under the Food, Drug and Cosmetic Act of 1938, the Food and Drug Administration (FDA) was granted powers analogous to those enjoyed by the CPSC under the CPSA. This means that duties to warn or recall prescription drugs and medical devices are also pre-empted, except in circumstances where a brand-name manufacturer learns of new dangers that are so significant that a new warning should be added to the product even before it receives FDA approval to do so. This pre-emption of a duty to warn leaves patients who consume *generic* drugs in a particularly precarious position. They cannot sue the generic manufacturer, since that is pre-empted, and in most states they also cannot sue the brand-name manufacturer (whether for defective design, failure to warn, or fraudulent concealment) because they did not consume the brand-name manufacturer's own product.

12.1.2 Agency Approaches

One type of conflict for which many self-styled "tort reformers" have often argued is so-called "field" pre-emption. This would mean that, if the federal government has legislated in any respect within a given field, state law would be pre-empted for the whole field. The courts have, however, consistently rejected this approach. Instead, they prefer to judge each case according to its own facts. Because products liability law is a matter for the states, it should be pre-empted only where the evidence clearly supports such a conclusion.

Indeed, that was, historically, precisely the approach of the federal agencies themselves. During the presidency of George W. Bush, however, they began to assert something akin to field pre-emption as a matter of course.

The FDA, for example, had made no claims that its existence pre-empted state tort law claims against pharmaceutical manufacturers until 2002. This new claim met with scathing criticism from, among others, a former FDA

Commissioner. President Barack Obama subsequently issued a memorandum to all federal agencies, reminding them of what federalism means and that

> [T]he citizens of the several States have distinctive circumstances and values, and that in many instances it is appropriate for them to apply to themselves rules and principles that reflect these circumstances and values.

Moreover, federal agencies only have the powers granted to them by legislation. They cannot unilaterally choose to go beyond them. Accordingly, the courts have grown wary of agencies' claims that whole fields of law are pre-empted and have instead re-emphasized the need for clear evidence of pre-emption in each case.

12.2 Mass Torts Litigation

Mass tort litigation involves a large number of plaintiffs with similar claims against the same (group of) defendants. Without intervention at the federal level, these could lead to large numbers of repetitious lawsuits that all need to be adjudicated individually for each specific plaintiff. This would not only waste considerable resources but also tie up the courts, thus causing even greater delays than those often experienced already.

Two significant approaches have, therefore, been adopted to ameliorate this issue: multi-district litigation (MDL) and class actions. Neither changes the substantive law involved, but they do create their own procedural requirements.

12.2.1 Multi-District Litigation

As its name suggests, multi-district litigation involves lawsuits being filed by different plaintiffs in different courts and jurisdictions, but against the same defendants. This risks not just a duplication of effort, causing unnecessary expenditure of time and resources, but also the possibility of a series of inconsistent rulings on matters of law and procedure which could cause wildly differing results from one jurisdiction to the next.

28 U.S.C. § 1407 seeks to avoid such issues by making it possible to consolidate pretrial proceedings for such cases by having them all transferred to one specific federal district. Such transfers may be initiated by the judicial panel

on multidistrict litigation upon its own initiative, or by the application of one of the parties.

12.2.2 Class Actions

As with MDLs, the idea of the device known as a "class action" is to avoid having the courts flooded with a huge number of cases which all involve the the same product and the same defendants. A class action requires certification by a judge in the jurisdiction where the action will be heard to say that the class fulfills the relevant requirements of the law.

So far as federal law is concerned, the certification of a class action is governed by Rule 23 of the Federal Rules of Procedure, which recognizes that such a class may comprise plaintiffs *or defendants*. The states have similar, if not identical, rules. Rule 23(a) provides:

> One or more members of a class may sue or be sued as representative parties on behalf of all members only if:
>
> 1. The class is so numerous that joinder of all members is impracticable;
> 3. There are questions of law or fact common to the class;
> 4. The claims or defenses of the representative parties are typical of the claims of defenses of the class; and
> 5. The representative parties will fairly and adequately protect the interests of the class.

Factor (2) is typically the one that weighs most heavily with the courts.

Where a class is certified, the Class Action Fairness Act of 2005 makes removal of a class action to federal court significantly more likely. The Act is seen as a "tort reform" measure, because the judiciary and the Federal Rules of Evidence (including those relating to the admission of expert witnesses) are perceived to be more defendant-friendly.

Recently, for example, the United States Court of Appeals for the Fourth Circuit addressed in *Shears v. Ethicon, Inc.*, 109 F.4th 235 (4th Cir. 2024), a class action brought by 37 women from West Virginia over alleged injuries caused by Tension-Free Vaginal Tape, manufactured by the defendant, Ethicon. After receiving a response from the Supreme Court of Appeals of West Virginia on points of West Virginia law that it had certified, however, the court vacated the trial court's judgment for the defendant and remanded for further proceedings.

Nevertheless, the judiciary—especially at the federal level—has generally become increasingly suspicious of class certification applications by plaintiffs. Their main cause for concern in terms of the legal requirements has been that proof of specific causation is very unlikely to involve evidence common to all the members of the class. Conversely, those seeking certification have tended to point out that questions of general causation *are* likely to be common to the whole class, and that it saves considerable time and expense if a class is certified, even if only for the purposes of resolving that issue.

However, many judges (and representatives of product manufacturers and distributors) have argued that class actions serve more as vehicles that benefit plaintiffs' attorneys than the plaintiffs themselves. They point, in particular, to so-called "coupon settlements," where each member of the class receives only a small sum of money—often in the form of a coupon or prepaid debit card—while their lawyers, on contingency fee, receive 30% plus of the total amount awarded to the whole class. The attorneys retort that, without such an incentive to represent claimants who have suffered relatively small injuries, there would be no deterrent effect, so that potential defendants would be free to manufacture and distribute defective products to their hearts' content.

12.3 Bankruptcy Protection

The purpose of bankruptcy protection law is to enable a fresh start for those who have fallen into severe financial difficulties. It also provides a means of avoiding unnecessary (financial) harm to those—like employees, customers, and suppliers—who depend on the business's survival. Ironically, however, there is no requirement in in the Bankruptcy Code itself for anyone entering bankruptcy protection to actually be insolvent or to be facing the prospect of imminent insolvency. There is, however, a requirement that filing for bankruptcy protection be done in good faith.

Title 11 of the United States Code denotes six different types of bankruptcy protection, but only two are significant for the purposes of products liability law. Chapter 7 bankruptcy brings an end to a corporation, gathers all the assets, and distributes them among all of its creditors. Successful products liability claimants then become just another unsecured creditor, which usually means that they will receive pennies on the dollar, if anything at all.

Chapter 11, on the other hand, allows businesses to petition for bankruptcy in order to reorganize and create a repayment plan designed to insure the company's long-term survival. Once the Bankruptcy Court has approved such a plan, they will be discharged from bankruptcy. Businesses often enter Chapter 11 bankruptcy protection with a "pre-packaged" re-organization plan already drawn up. The most controversial form of pre-packaged bankruptcy has become known as the "Texas Two-Step," which has been widely criticized as an abuse of the bankruptcy system designed only to prevent products liability victims recovering their rightful compensation.

A Texas Two-Step bankruptcy involves a solvent parent company spinning off its liabilities for a defective product into a new company, which then declares a Chapter 11 bankruptcy. The parent company then asks the Bankruptcy Court for a release of all liabilities it assigned to its spinoff. If granted, litigants are then limited to pursuing recourse only against the spinoff, which has limited funds to meet compensation claims, while the parent company continues to operate normally.

Courts have, however, recently shown a greater readiness to police the Texas Two-Step (and other petitions for bankruptcy protection), where the entity in question is not in "financial distress," on the grounds that lack of such distress demonstrates a lack of good faith.

12.3.1 Automatic Stay

Even apart from a Texas Two-Step bankruptcy, a major attraction for any entity entering bankruptcy protection is that any legal claim against it is automatically and immediately stayed under 11 U.S.C. § 362. This means that current claims are suspended indefinitely and removed to the Bankruptcy Court, unless that court expressly permits a lawsuit to continue.

Any new claims are also automatically stayed, as are any judgments entered up to 90 days before the date of filing. Indeed, defendants to a products liability lawsuit sometimes threaten that they will enter Chapter 11 bankruptcy precisely in order to nullify any award against them if litigation is pursued. But it is not only plaintiffs who may be impacted if a defendant takes such a course of action. Any co-defendants who do not also enter Chapter 11 bankruptcy may find themselves saddled with significantly greater compensation liabilities, especially in jurisdictions that recognize joint and several liability.

It is worth emphasizing that the automatic stay applies to pre-petition product *defects*, not pre-petition products. This has particularly serious implications for design defects, since a product with such a defect may be sold or otherwise distributed years after the design was completed. A victim may thus also be injured years after the design was approved by the defendant, and so be injured well after the defendant was discharged from bankruptcy protection. Yet if the product was designed before the defendant *entered* bankruptcy protection, any claim arising out of a design defect will still be automatically stayed.

12.3.2 Liability Insurance

An additional ramification of a business entering bankruptcy is often overlooked. In most jurisdictions, a business will be obliged by law to have some form of liability insurance, which would be expected to meet (albeit only up to coverage limits) any financial award made against the policy-holder by a court. Moreover, the automatic stay does not apply to claims brought directly against an insurer.

Most states, however, prohibit the bringing of suits directly against a defendant's liability insurer unless the insurer has colluded in the commission of a tort (typically fraudulent concealment). But the real problem for victims of defective products arises from the practice of many large businesses to "self-insure" the first hundred(s) of thousands of dollars of potential liability. This is generally known as a "self-insured retention" (SIR).

This means that the liability insurer will come "on risk" only if a claim exceeds the amount that the policy-holder has chosen to self-insure. For this reason, this type of insurance is typically known as "excess" liability insurance. It is much less expensive to obtain because the insurers are much less likely to be called upon to pay out.

The problem this creates for victims of defective products manufactured or distributed by the policy-holder is twofold. The power to claim any amount up to the limit of the SIR will be automatically stayed by that policy-holder petitioning for bankruptcy protection. Once the stay is in place, that money will not be paid. But because this means that the SIR will not be exhausted, then the excess insurance policy cannot be triggered, and so the victim will receive nothing from the liability insurer either.

Courts are sometimes prepared to skirt around this problem by treating an SIR as if it were a policy deductible, so that the excess insurance can then be triggered without the need to exhaust the SIR, but this very much depends on how each individual liability insurance policy is worded.

ROLE OF FEDERAL LAW CHECKPOINTS

- The courts recognize express and implied pre-emption, but not field pre-emption.
- Multi-district litigation involves consolidating pretrial proceedings by transferring cases to a specific district court.
- Class actions are more likely to be removed to federal court, but are increasingly disfavored by the judiciary.
- A defendant who enters bankruptcy protection will trigger an automatic stay of any liabilities against it that arise from pre-petition product defects.
- A defendant in bankruptcy protection who maintained a self-insured retention (SIR) will also relieve its liability insurer of the obligation to meet any pre-petition product defect liabilities unless a court decides to threat the SIR as equivalent to a policy deductible.

CHAPTER 13

Damages

DAMAGES ROADMAP

- Understand the different types of damages awards
- Understand the different types of harm for which damages may be awarded

---

13.1 Types of Damages

While it is sometimes true that plaintiffs in products liability cases may seek to have sales of a defective product banned, or to have such products recalled, by far the most common remedy sought is financial recompense for the harm caused. Such compensation is known as compensatory damages. But compensatory damages are not the only form of damages available. In fact, the law recognizes three different types of damages. These are:

- Nominal Damages
- Compensatory Damages
- Punitive Damages

13.1.1 Nominal Damages

Nominal damages—typically one dollar—are awarded when the plaintiff has shown that the theory of the case for which they argued has been shown to be correct, but no real loss has been suffered. The law still treats the case as a victory for the plaintiff but it says, in effect, that the litigation was a waste of time. It is extremely rare for a products liability case to end with an award of nominal damages.

13.1.2 Compensatory Damages

As noted above, by far the most common remedy awarded is compensatory damages. These attempt to compensate the victim by awarding them a sum of money equivalent either to the cost of repair or to the loss of value suffered. Such damages may cover several different types of harm, namely:

- Property Damage
- Personal Injury
- Economic Loss
- Emotional Distress

In addition, a successful plaintiff may also seek to claim punitive damages. These are not intended to compensate the victim for harm sustained but, as their name suggests, to punish the defendant for acting (or failing to act) in a particularly egregious manner.

13.2 Property Damage

Damages to compensate for loss of, or harm to, property are the easiest to assess. For a start, loss or damage to property is easy to verify objectively. The size of monetary awards to compensate for such loss or harm is also susceptible to objective calculation. The cost of repair is typically based on actual receipts for the work, while an award for loss of value will involve a market value appraisal which, while likely to be less specific than a receipt for repair, will involve the use of generally-agreed methods or tools to arrive at the valuation.

The one thing that must be remembered when addressing property damage is that it does not include harm to the defective product itself. As has been noted several times in this book, such harm is properly categorized as economic loss.

13.3 Personal Injury

At first glance, damages awarded to compensate for personal injuries might also seem unproblematic. External personal injuries are clearly visible and may be recorded in photographs or videos. Even when they are internal, injuries can typically be verified with images generated by scans and X-rays.

But while their existence may be easily verified, the amount of compensation to be paid for them is not so clear-cut. As in the case of property damage, compensatory damages awards for personal injury are intended to reflect either loss of value or the cost of repair. It might be thought that receipts for medical bills represent the latter and, in principle, this is correct. But the position when a medical care provider offers a discount to holders of certain medical insurance policies muddies the waters, because it is not clear whether the original "sticker" price or the discounted price provides the better basis for the amount of money to be paid in compensation.

And what of the loss of (say) a limb, or an eye? There is no obvious way of calculating how much should be paid in compensation in either case. The victim will present evidence of how such losses have affected their life, but it will be impossible for anyone to arrive at an objectively-verifiable dollar amount that should be paid in compensation. In the case of loss of life, wrongful death statutes specify that the amount to be paid should be based on the loss of financial support suffered by the decedent's dependents.

Awards for pain and suffering have proved particularly problematic. Even if a brain scan can sometimes clearly objectively verify the existence of the victim's pain, there is simply no way that the significance of that pain can be properly identified. (Doctors often ask patients to rate their pain on a scale of 1 to 10, but everyone's experiences and pain thresholds are different.) And even if it were possible to calculate the amount of pain, it would still be a subjective judgment as to how much money should be awarded to compensate for each pain increment.

13.3.1 Loss of Consortium

Compensatory damages for loss of consortium present a similar problem but for a different plaintiff. While loss of consortium is treated as a form of physical injury, it is not a loss sustained by the primary victim. Instead, it represents the loss of companionship and mentoring suffered by those in close relationships with the primary victim.

Again, however, it is hard to know how to value such relationships in monetary terms. Sometimes it is possible to point to the cost of hiring a professional replacement (e.g., the cost of hiring a nanny after the death of a parent), but relationships are surely much more valuable than the purely practical services that they often provide.

13.4 Economic Loss

In a practical sense, economic losses are the easiest to compensate, since both the losses and the compensation for them are calculated by the same financial metric. In legal terms, however, economic losses are problematic because there are two different types, namely:

- Consequential economic loss
- Pure economic loss

The law treats these two types differently.

13.4.1 Consequential Economic Loss

Damages for economic losses consequential on physical harm are essentially uncontroversial. They can usually be objectively verified and even if, as with a loss of future income, they require predictions of the future, recognized actuarial conventions mean that there will typically be relatively little dispute about the amounts of money involved. (There might be disputes over the medical prognosis on which the calculations are based, but those are not disputes about the method of calculation.)

13.4.2 Pure Economic Loss

Stand-alone, or "pure," economic losses are a very different matter. This is not because they are harder to verify objectively. In fact, there will typically be no greater difficulty involved in evaluating pure economic losses than consequential economic losses.

The problem from the law's point of view is that allowing recovery for pure economic losses risks adding significantly to the number of plaintiffs who might then successfully bring a claim. It might seem counter-intuitive that a defendant who causes harm to more people should be insulated from (some of) the resultant claims for compensation, while a defendant who injures just one or two people should bear the full cost of the compensation burden. But, as noted in Chapter 1, the law is wary of the potential for floods of lawsuits.

Claims of compensation for harm done to the defective product itself are a form of pure economic loss that the law does treat as recoverable—but only as part of a claim for breach of warranty within the law of contracts. The reason for this is that a contract significantly limits the scope of who can bring a claim. Only a party who has privity of contract with the defendant will be permitted to succeed.

The same reasoning applies more broadly too. As explained in Chapter 3, victims of misrepresentation may sometimes be able to bring a claim for compensation for pure economic loss—but, once again, only if they have a contract with the representor. Otherwise a victim will need to show some form of personal injury or property damage resulted from the misrepresentation; if proved, that would then permit an additional claim for any *consequential* economic losses. Claims for *pure* economic loss in torts other than misrepresentation are extremely unlikely to succeed.

13.5 Emotional Distress

Claims seeking compensation for emotional distress have proved most problematic of all. They can be subdivided into two, one of which can itself also be subdivided into two. The initial subcategories are:

- Primary victims
- Secondary victims

13.5.1 Primary Victims

Primary victims are those who suffer emotional distress without a predicate injury to someone else. Someone who loses a limb, for example, is almost certain to suffer significant emotional distress in additional to the personal injury. But primary victims may suffer one of two different types of emotional distress, namely:

- Consequential emotional distress
- Pure emotional distress

13.5.1.1 Consequential Emotional Distress

The law treats such consequential emotional distress in much the same way as it treats consequential economic loss. While it does increase the total sum of compensation to be awarded, it does not increase the number of plaintiffs bringing a claim and so cannot potentially cause a flood of lawsuits.

Instead, the main problem with such claims lies in working out how much money should be awarded since there is no way to objectively calculate the amount of distress. But this is really no greater a problem than calculating compensatory damages for personal injuries.

13.5.1.2 Pure Emotional Distress

As noted in chapter 6, however, claims for emotional distress that are *not* predicated on personal injury have typically been rejected by the courts. By contrast with consequential emotional distress claims, these do potentially create the risk of a flood of lawsuits. Moreover, without a predicate injury and an objectively-reliable set of tests for determining whether someone really is suffering from emotional distress, the courts have been concerned to avoid the possibility of fraudulent claims.

As a consequence, pure emotional distress suffered by primary victims is recoverable only in negligence claims.

13.5.2 Secondary Victims

This reluctance to permit claims for pure emotional distress by primary victims is multiplied in the case of claims brought by secondary victims. These are people who suffer emotional distress after witnessing a primary victim being physically harmed by a defective product. Products liability law will not entertain such claims unless a case of negligence can be made out. Otherwise, if a secondary victim wishes to bring a lawsuit, they will need to satisfy the criteria for a claim of loss of consortium.

13.6 Punitive Damages

As their name suggests, punitive damages are awarded not to compensate the victim but to punish the defendant. By making an example of the defendant, it is hoped that they will also deter others from engaging in similar conduct in the future. This, it is said, enables ordinary citizens (and their attorneys) to act like private attorneys-general in holding the manufacturers and distributors of defective products to account.

To justify such punishment, however, the defendant must have engaged in particularly egregious behavior. This requires, at the very least, a conscious disregard for a known, substantial, and unjustifiable risk.

Punitive damages are, accordingly, not awarded for a defendant's breach of warranty, since contractual liability is strict and therefore involves no finding about the defendant's state of mind. Manufacturing defects, too, involve strict liability and so do not lend themselves to an award of punitive damages unless it can be established that the defendant knew of the risk of such defects but recklessly chose to ignore it.

Even negligence does not normally warrant punishment. While such behavior is unreasonable, it is typically accompanied by a *lack* of thought rather than conscious disregard.

By contrast, there are cases where an award of punitive damages is virtually inevitable. These involve intentional wrongdoing, such as fraudulent misrepresentation or fraudulent concealment. Design defect cases where the defendant knew of an alternative reasonable design but decided not to adopt it may also result in punitive damages awards, especially if the reason for failing to adopt the alternative was to save a rather small amount of money.

13.6.1 Guidance for Juries

The main problem with punitive damages awards is that they are awarded not by the judge but by a jury. This contrasts sharply with a criminal prosecution, which is the principal legal forum for meting out punishment. There it is the role of the judge to pronounce sentence, and judges have sentencing guidelines to assist them in working out the appropriate sanction. Moreover, that is part of a judge's job: they gain experience in sentencing criminals. But juries have no such experience, and the common law has traditionally provided the jury with no guidance on how to calculate the amount of such an award. This has inevitably led to the amounts of punitive damages awarded being highly unpredictable.

To supporters of punitive damages, however, this very unpredictability is the strength of punitive damages; it is the very fear of a huge award that acts as a big deterrent to wrongdoing.

13.6.2 Supreme Court Guidance

While the US Supreme Court has insisted that the common law of contracts and torts is a matter for the states, it has also asserted itself to be the ultimate arbiter of the limits of a punitive damages award. Despite memorable dissents from the late Justice Scalia, who argued strongly that punitive damages awards were none of the Court's business, a majority has repeatedly declared over the last thirty years or so that its power derives from the Due Process Clause of the Fourteenth Amendment.

The Court has pursued two objectives. One is to eradicate awards of punitive damages that take into account harm caused to victims who are not a party to the lawsuit at hand. The other is to eliminate "grossly excessive" punitive damages awards.

Recognizing that unpredictability is an essential part of the deterrence function of punitive damages, the Court has been reluctant to specify with great precision the outer limits of such awards, but it seems quite clear that they should not amount to a sum that is ten or more times the total of compensatory damages awarded. Double digit multipliers are clearly out of bounds. But in most cases, it seems that the Court will eye with suspicion any multiplier over 4. It is not clear why this should be the magic number but, once the Court insists that there must be an outer limit, it must have a number in mind. Whatever number is chosen is always going to be arbitrary.

13.6.3 Likelihood of Payment

It is important to stress, however, that punitive damages awards are rarely paid. It is not just that relatively few successful torts claims result in such awards; it needs also to be emphasized that only around two percent *of those cases* actually end with the award intact. Thus, only around one in a thousand successful plaintiffs actually gets to receive a punitive damages award.

The reason is that any punitive damages award will almost automatically be met by the defendant deciding to appeal. This can lead to years of protracted litigation, whose outcome is difficult to predict. In reality, it is probably better to see an award of punitive damages as opening a new stage of negotiations between the parties, with the plaintiff often prepared to accept a much smaller sum immediately on the basis that a bird in the hand is worth two (or, perhaps, twenty) in the bush, and with the defendant often prepared to pay such a reduced sum in order to get closure on the case (and, where the agreement is confidential, without any indication to other, prospective plaintiffs that a similar suit will necessarily be worthwhile).

13.6.4 Racketeer Influenced and Corrupt Organizations (RICO) Act

The Racketeer Influenced and Corrupt Organizations (RICO) Act is principally concerned with criminal activity. It does, however, contain provisions, 18 U.S.C. § 1962(b), 1964(c), that expressly permit civil actions to be brought against persons who engage in a "pattern of racketeering activity" that causes harm to "business or property." Moreover, a successful plaintiff in such a suit is entitled, 18 U.S.C. § 1964(c), to "recover threefold the damages he sustains and the cost of the suit, including a reasonable attorney's fee."

A "pattern of racketeering activity" involves at least two prohibited acts within ten years of each other. The statute lists the acts it regards as prohibited. For the purposes of products liability law, the most significant are mail fraud and wire fraud. So, if a plaintiff can prove a manufacturer or distributor of a defective product used the telephone or mail at least twice to discuss the defect, a RICO action may be available, even if the use of the mail or telephone was for purely intra-corporate communication. There is no requirement that the telephone or mail be the instrument of wire or mail fraud, so long as they were involved in the furtherance of the fraud.

While the requirement for harm to "business or property" rules out the possibility of using a RICO claim where the injury suffered is personal injury, it can be a powerful tool in a case where the plaintiff has suffered property damage (provided, of course, that such damage is not damage to the defective product itself). It is especially powerful because there is no requirement that the defendant must first have been convicted of a criminal offense.

RICO has previously been used against cigarette manufacturers who fraudulently agreed among themselves to conceal their knowledge that smoking causes cancer. Currently before the US Supreme Court is a case that presents an ingenious argument. The plaintiff took a hemp-derived CBD product, advertised as THC-free, to treat chronic pain. But the product did contain THC and he failed a routine drug test at work, causing him to be fired. The Second Circuit Court of Appeals, *Horn v. Medical Marijuana, Inc.*, 80 F.4th 130 (2d Cir. 2023), considered this to be a potential case of mail and wire fraud, causing injury to his business or property. The Supreme Court seems likely to disagree; otherwise the use of RICO is likely to expand significantly in future products liability cases.

DAMAGES CHECKPOINTS

Damages may be classified in many ways:

- Nominal Damages
- Compensatory Damages
    - Property Damage: recoverable in all products liability claims
    - Personal Injury: recoverable in all products liability claims
        - Pain and Suffering
        - Loss of Consortium
    - Economic Loss
        - Consequential Economic Loss: recoverable in all products liability claims
        - Pure Economic Loss: recoverable only in misrepresentation and breach of warranty claims
    - Emotional Distress
        - Primary Victims
            - Consequential Emotional Distress: recoverable in all products liability claims
            - Pure Emotional Distress: recoverable only in negligence claims
        - Secondary Victims: recoverable only in negligence claims
- Punitive Damages
- Triple damages under the Racketeer Influenced and Corrupt Organizations (RICO) Act (and attorneys' fees)

Mastering Products Liability Checklist

The following reflects the topics covered in each chapter. A thorough understanding and knowledge of each of the items mentioned will be necessary for a good background in Products Liability.

CHAPTER 1 • HISTORY AND BACKGROUND OF PRODUCTS LIABILITY

- ☐ Fundamental to products liability law is the distinction between a product and a service.
- ☐ Modern products liability law grew out of the inadequacies of the laws on breach of warranty, misrepresentation, and negligence.

CHAPTER 2 • WARRANTIES

- ☐ Warranties may be express or implied.
- ☐ Implied warranties comprise those of merchantability and of fitness for purpose.

CHAPTER 3 • MISREPRESENTATION

- ☐ Misrepresentations involve an untrue statement of fact or expert opinion that is not puffery and that was relied on by the representee to their detriment.
- ☐ A misrepresentation may be intentional, conscious, negligent, or innocent.

CHAPTER 4 • NEGLIGENCE

- ☐ Negligence requires that the plaintiff prove duty of care, breach of duty, causation, and harm.
- ☐ *Res ipsa loquitur* may enable the drawing of an inference of breach of duty and/or specific causation.

CHAPTER 5 • SECOND VS THIRD RESTATEMENTS

- ☐ A major controversy continues to haunt products liability over whether to apply section 402A of the Second Restatement of Torts or the Products Liability Restatement.
- ☐ The Second Restatement is seen as more plaintiff-friendly; the Products Liability Restatement is seen as more defendant-friendly and an example of so-called "tort reform."

CHAPTER 6 • MANUFACTURING DEFECTS

- ☐ The test for a manufacturing defect in food is either the foreign-natural or the consumer expectations test.
- ☐ A manufacturing defect exists in other products when a product fails to meet consumer expectations (Second Restatement) or differs from the intended design (Third Restatement).

CHAPTER 7 • DESIGN DEFECTS

- ☐ A design defect exists in other products when a product fails to meet consumer expectations (Second Restatement) or fails the risk-utility test (Third Restatement).
- ☐ Within the risk-utility test, proof of a reasonable alternative design may be required, or it may be one of several factors involved.
- ☐ The reasonable alternative design requirement is inapplicable to prescription drugs and rarely applicable to medical devices.
- ☐ A product that was manufactured according to the state of the art at the time will not be considered to have a design defect.
- ☐ Remedial measures implemented after someone is injured cannot typically be used as evidence that the product design at the time was defective.

CHAPTER 8 • FAILURES TO WARN

- ☐ Whether there is a duty to warn will depend on the consumer expectations test (Second Restatement) or the risk-utility test (Third Restatement).
- ☐ If there is a duty to warn, the warning must be conspicuous, inform the user of the risks and their likely severity, and provide a reasonable means for the user to manage, contain, or avoid the risks.
- ☐ The test of reasonableness is modified for a sophisticated user and for a learned intermediary.

CHAPTER 9 • CAUSATION

- ☐ General causation is a matter of law on which a judge should rule. It considers whether the product defect is capable of causing the type of harm alleged.
- ☐ General causation in toxic torts claims relies heavily on epidemiological evidence.
- ☐ Specific causation is a matter of fact for the jury to decide according to the but-for test, the substantial factor test, or by inference from known facts.

CHAPTER 10 • EXPERT EVIDENCE

- ☐ There is a split among the states about the test for admissibility of expert evidence.
- ☐ The majority of states and the federal system favor the *Daubert* test and Rule 702 of the Federal Rules of Evidence, which involves weighing a number of factors.
- ☐ A minority of jurisdictions continue to favor the *Frye* test, which asks whether the evidence presented is generally accepted in the particular field to which it belongs.

CHAPTER 11 • AFFIRMATIVE DEFENSES

- ☐ Defenses based on the victim's own conduct are contributory negligence, comparative fault, comparative causation, and failure to mitigate.
- ☐ Government contractors may also enjoy immunity for design defects and failures to warn.
- ☐ Defenses based on the lapse of time involve statutes of limitation and statutes of repose.

CHAPTER 12 • ROLE OF FEDERAL LAW

- ☐ The courts recognize express and implied pre-emption, but not field pre-emption.
- ☐ Multi-district litigation involves consolidating pretrial proceedings by transferring cases to a specific district court.
- ☐ A defendant who enters bankruptcy protection will trigger an automatic stay of any liabilities against it that arise from pre-petition product defects.
- ☐ A defendant in bankruptcy protection who maintained a self-insured retention (SIR) will also relieve its liability insurer of the obligation to meet any pre-petition product defect liabilities unless a court decides to threat the SIR as equivalent to a policy deductible.

CHAPTER 13 • DAMAGES

- ☐ Compensatory damages for personal injury and property damage are recoverable in all products liability claims.
- ☐ Compensatory damages for consequential economic loss are recoverable in all products liability claims, but compensatory damages for pure economic loss are recoverable only in misrepresentation and breach of warranty claims.
- ☐ Compensatory damages for consequential emotional distress of the primary victim are recoverable in all products liability claims, but compensatory damages for pure emotional distress (whether of primary or secondary victims) are recoverable only in negligence claims.
- ☐ Punitive damages—and triple damages under the Racketeer Influenced and Corrupt Organizations (RICO) Act—may also be available.

Index